4·00

Orthodox Spirituality

This edition is offered from the translator
to the Birth of the Theotokos monastery

Original title: Mikra Isodos stin Orthodoxi Pnevmatikotita

First published in 1992 by the Apostoliki Diakonia editions
to which many thanks are due for their kind permission
to proceed with this translation.

Published by: Birth of the Theotokos Monastery
               P.O. 107, 321 00 Levadia, Greece
               Tel. & Fax: 0268 31204

First edition 1994

Reprinted 1996, 1998

ISBN 960-7070-20-8

**Metropolitan of Nafpaktos
Hierotheos**

Orthodox Spirituality
a brief introduction

translated by
Effie Mavromichali

Birth of the Theotokos Monastery

Contents

Translator's Preface

Under the title "Orthodox Spirituality" the author of this book wishes to present the fundamentals of Orthodox spiritual life.

He delineates, in a very concise manner, the boundaries of Orthodox ecclesiastical life by redefining terms long misused or misinterpreted: praxis, theoria, nous, reason, cure of the soul etc.

Rather, the author tries to reorientate our mind and thus our life to the authentic word and empirical theology of the Fathers.

What is made clear is that Orthodox Spirituality is not meant as abstract knowledge, which has to be mastered rationally, but as a mode of life, which embodies man's salvation – his communion and union with the Holy Trinity God.

This undertaking has been completed thanks to the wholehearted offer and generous help of Virginia Chryssikos. I am indebted to her for having checked my translation.

Errors and omissions remain the translator's.

Effie Mavromichali

Preface

It has been noted that the theology of the Orthodox Church has passed through its own "Babylonian captivity", i.e. to the theology of the West, at least for a certain period of time. This is not said of the authentic theology of our Church but refers to the influence that the bearers of Orthodox theology had undergone.

This influence can be seen mainly in the way that certain aspects of truth have been formulated and then expressed. An example is the issue of the concept of "satisfaction of Divine Justice"; it upholds the view that original sin is inherited guilt transferred from generation to generation; there is also the secularization of life within the Church, in theological discourse and pastoral care etc.; it could be said that the Orthodox people have not been as significantly affected by the theology of the West, since the majority of the faithful have remained true to the following of Orthodox tradition.

Presently, a significant effort is being made in the search for and experiencing of the essence of the Orthodox Church. All theological writing as well as the way of life of the Orthodox faithful aim at this goal. Sermons, pastoral service, philanthropic acts, charitable offerings and all other activities within the Church are all manifestations of how Holy Orthodox tradition permeats all aspects of living for the Orthodox Christian. Barlaamism as an expression and way of life is gradually being expelled from Orthodoxy. Studies and publications of patristic works are rekindling the interest in Orthodox, ecclesiastical life and leading to a rediscovering of its spirituality.

However, it is quite necessary for the fundamentals of the Orthodox spiritual life to be defined, because of the frequent reference made to the teachings of the Fathers and because to a certain extent, the interpretation of these teachings has been subjected to the Western theological view, i.e. some aspects of patristic teaching have been misinterpreted. This is the case with the terms "praxis" and "theoria", which are very often employed but understood within the dialectic of the West. And it is indeed an error not to place and redefine such terms within the milieu of Orthodox tradition. The contents of this present book offer a brief introduction to Orthodox spirituality. It is not the author's purpose to analyse the subject comprehensively, but rather his intention is to introduce on a "small entry" the domain of Orthodox, ecclesiastical tradition.

I must notice that the meaning of the term "spirituality" is better rendered by the phrase "spiritual life", because it is not an abstract condition being referred to –as is understood in the West– but rather it is the energy of the Holy Spirit within the person. However, the term "spirituality" is used in this book somewhat conventionally, so that by analysing it, a place is given to it within Orthodox tradition, whereby it can be distinguished from other non-hypostatic spiritual traditions. In this way, on the one hand, a point of reference is offered to the contemporary man –who is more familiar with this term– and at the same time, the author is afforded the opportunity to delineate the boundaries of this term within Orthodox tradition. The basic elements of Orthodox spirituality are presented in a simple way, in this book. Large numbers of quotations have been avoided so that the reader does not find the book too tedious. Yet, whoever is interested in more in depth analysis of the themes treated in this text can refer to other books written by this author.

This present work is a "small entry", a brief introduction. May the reader seize the opportunity to make his own "great entry" to the spirituality of the Orthodox tradition.

1. Defining Orthodox Spirituality

It is necessary first to define the terms: "orthodox" and "spirituality". We cannot speak about "Orthodox spirituality" unless we know exactly what we mean by these two words. This is what the Holy Fathers of the Church have done. In his exceptional book "The Source of knowledge", and more specifically in the sections entitled "Philosophical Chapters", St. John of Damascus analyses the meanings of these words: Substance, nature, hypostasis, person etc. Because these terms can be defined differently whitin other contexts he explains why they are so defined here.

The adjective "orthodox" comes from the noun "orthodoxy" and shows the difference between the Orthodox Church and every other Christian denomination. The word "Orthodoxy" manifests the true knowledge about God and creation. This is the definition St. Anastasios of Sinai offers[1]

The term Orthodoxy consists of two words: "orthi" (ὀρθή = true, right) and "doxa". "Doxa" (δόξα) means, on the one hand, belief, faith, teaching and on the other, praise or doxology. These two meanings are closely connected. The true teaching about God incorporates the true praise of God; for if God is abstract, then prayer to this God is abstract as well. If God is

---

1. See PG 89, 76 D.

personal then prayer assumes a personal character. God has revealed the true faith, the true teaching. Thus we say that the teaching about God and all matters associated with a person's salvation are the Revelation of God and not man's discovery.

God has revealed this truth to people who were prepared to receive it. Judas expresses this point well by saying: "contend for the faith which was once delivered unto the saints" (Judas, 3). In this quotation as in many other related passages it is clear that God reveals Himself to the Saints, i.e. to those who have reached a certain level of spiritual growth so as to receive this Revelation. The Holy Apostles were "healed" first, and then received the Revelation. And they transmitted this Revelation to their spiritual children not only by teaching them but primarily by mystically effecting their spiritual rebirth. In order for this faith to be preserved the Holy Fathers formulated the dogmas and doctrines. We accept the dogmas and doctrines; in other words we accept this revealed faith and remain within the Church so as to be healed. For faith is, on the one hand, Revelation to those purified and healed and, on the other it is the right path to reach theosis, for those who choose to follow the "way".

The word "spirituality" (pnevmaticotis - πνευματι-κότης) comes from "spiritual" (pnevmatikos - πνευμα-τικός). Thus, spirituality is the state of the spiritual person. Spiritual man has a certain way of behaving, a certain mentality. He acts differently from the way non-spiritual people behave.

The spirituality of the Orthodox Church, however, does not lead to abstract religious life; nor is it the fruits of man's inner strength. Spirituality is not an abstract religious life because the Church is the Body of Christ. It is not simply a religion which believes in a God, theoretically. The Second Person of the Holy Trinity -the Logos of God- assumed human nature for us. He united it with his hypostasis and became the Head of the Church.

Thus the Church is the Body of the Godman Christ. Moreover, spirituality is not a manifestation of the energies of the soul as reason is, or the feelings are etc. This is important to state because many people tend to label a person spiritual who cultivates his reasoning abilities: a scientist, an artist, an actor, a poet etc. This interpretation is not accepted by the Orthodox Church. Certainly we are not against scientists, poets etc., but we cannot call them spiritual people in the strict orthodox sense of the word.

In the teaching of the Apostle Paul the spiritual man is clearly distinguished from the man of the soul. Spiritual is the man who has the energy of the Holy Spirit within. Whereas the man of the soul is he who has body and soul but has not acquired the Holy Spirit, which gives life to the soul. "But the natural man receiveth not the things of the Spirit of God: for they are foolishness unto him: neither can he know them, because they are spiritually discerned. But he that is spiritual judgeth all things, yet he himself is judged of no man" (1 Cor. 2, 14-15).

In the same Epistle, the Apostle Paul draws the distinction between the spiritual man and the man of the flesh. The man of the flesh is he who does not have the Holy Spirit within his heart but retains all the other psychosomatic functions of a human being. Therefore it is evident that the term "man of the flesh" does not refer to the body, but signifies the man of the soul who lacks the Most Holy Spirit, and who operates out of his so called "psychobiological" self. "And I, brethren, could not speak unto you as unto spiritual, but as unto carnal, even as unto babes in Christ. I have fed you with milk, and not with meat: for hitherto ye were not able to bear it, neither yet now are ye able. For ye are yet carnal: for whereas there is among you envying, and strife, and divisions, are ye not carnal, and walk as men?" (1 Cor. 3, 1-3).

If we combine the above mentioned passages with those referring to the Christians' adoption by grace, we ascertain that, according to the Apostle Paul, spiritual is the man who by grace has become son of God. "Therefore, brethren, we are debtors, not to the flesh, to live after the flesh. For if ye live after the flesh, ye shall die: but if ye through the Spirit do mortify the deeds of the body, ye shall live. For as many as are led by the Spirit of God, they are the sons of God. For ye have not received the spirit of bondage again to fear; but ye have received the Spirit of adoption, whereby we cry, Abba, Father. The Spirit itself beareth witness with our spirit, that we are the children of God" (Rom. 8, 12-16).

Spiritual is the man who is witness to the Holy Spirit within his heart and is thus well aware of the indwelling of the Holy Triune God. In this way he realizes that he is son of God by grace; and within his heart therefore, he cries "Abba, Father". According to the testimony of the Saints this heartfelt cry is essentially the noetic prayer or prayer of the heart.

St. Basil the Great in examining what is meant by "man becomes the temple of the Most Holy Spirit", teaches –inspired by God– that the man who is the Temple of the Holy Spirit is not disturbed by temptations and constant cares; he seeks God and has communion with Him. Clearly the spiritual man is he who has the Holy Spirit within and this is confirmed by his uninterrupted remembrance of God[2].

According to St. Gregory Palamas, just as the man endowed with reason is called rational, in the same way the man who is enriched with the Holy Spirit is called spiritual. Thus spiritual is the "new man"; the regenerated by the grace of the Most Holy Spirit.

This same outlook is shared by all of the Holy Fathers. St. Symeon the New Theologian, for example, says that the man who is prudent, forbearing and meek, and who prays and beholds God, "walks in the spirit". He is pre-eminently the spiritual man, par excellence.

Again according to St. Symeon the New Theologian, when the parts of man's soul –his nous* and intellect– are not "clothed" in the image of Christ, he is considered a man of the flesh, since he does not have the sense of spiritual glory. The man of the flesh is like the blind person who cannot see the light from the sun's rays. In fact he is considered both blind and lifeless. In contrast, the spiritual man, who partakes in the energies of the Holy Spirit, is alive in God[3].

---

2. See St. Basil the Great, Greek Fathers of the Church (in Greek, E.Π.E.), Thessaloniki 1972, Vol. 1, p. 68

3. See SC 51, 54, vγ′

*Nous: The word has various uses in Patristic teaching. It indicates either the soul or the heart or even and energy of the soul. Yet, the nous is mainly the eye of the soul; the purest part of the soul; the highest attention. It is also called noetic energy and it is not identified with reason.

As we emphasized, previously, communion in the Most Holy Spirit makes the man of the flesh spiritual. For this reason, according to Orthodox teaching, the spiritual man, par excellence, is the Saint. Certainly, this is said from the point of view that a Saint is he who partakes, in varying degrees, in the uncreated grace of God, and especially in the deifying energy of God.

The Saints are bearers and manifestations of Orthodox spirituality. They live in God and consecutively they speak about Him. In this sense, Orthodox spirituality is not abstracted but is embodied in the personhood of the Saints. Hence the Saints are not the good people, the moralists in the strict sense of the term, or simply those who are good natured. Rather, saint is the person who submits to and acts upon the guidance of the Most Holy Spirit within.

We are assured of the existence of the Saints firstly by their Orthodox teaching. The Saints received and are receiving the Revelation of God; they experience it and they formulate it. They are the infallible criteria of the Ecumenical Synods. The second assurance is the existence of holy relics of the Saints. The holy relics are the token that through the nous the grace of God transfigured the body also. Consequently, the bodies participate in the energies of the Most Holy Spirit.

The primary work of the Church is to lead man to theosis, to communion and union with God. Given this, in a sense we can say that the work of the Church is to "produce relics".

Thus, Orthodox spirituality is the experience of life in Christ, the atmosphere of the new man, regenerated by the grace of God. It is not an abstract, emotional and psychological state of being. It is man's union with God.

Within this framework we can detect some characteristic traits of Orthodox spirituality. It is firstly Christ-centred, since Christ is the one and only "remedy" for people, by virtue of the hypostatic unity of the divine and human nature in His person. Secondly, Orthodox spirituality is Holy Trinity-centred, since Christ is always united with the Father and the Holy Spirit. All the sacraments are performed in the name of the Triune God. Being the Head of the Church, Christ cannot be thought of as being outside of it. Consequently Orthodox spirituality is also Ecclesiastic-centred, since only within the Church can we come into communion with Christ. Finally, as we shall explain later, Orthodox spirituality is mystical and ascetical.

2. Difference between Orthodox Spirituality and other Traditions

What we have said up to this point clearly indicates that Orthodox spirituality differs distinctly from any other "spirituality" of an eastern or western type. There can be no confusion among the various spiritualities, because Orthodox spirituality is Theanthropic centred, whereas all others are man-centred.

The difference appears primarily in the doctrinal teaching. For this reason we put "Orthodox" before the word "Church" so as to distinguish it from any other religion. Certainly "Orthodox" must be linked with the term "Ecclesiastic", since Orthodoxy cannot exist outside of the Church; neither, of course, can the Church exist outside Orthodoxy.

The dogmas are the results of decisions made at the Ecumenical Councils on various matters of faith. Dogmas are referred to as such, because they draw the boundaries between truth and error, between sickness and health. Dogmas express the revealed truth. They formulate the life of the Church. Thus they are, on the one hand, the expression of Revelation and on the other act as "remedies" in order to lead us to communion with God; to our reason for being.

Dogmatic differences reflect corresponding differences in therapy. If a person does not follow the "right way" he cannot ever reach his destination. If he does not take the proper "remedies", he cannot ever acquire health; in other words, he will experience no therapeutic benefits. Again, if we compare Orthodox spirituality with other Christian traditions, the difference in approach and method of therapy is more evident. A fundamental teaching of the Holy Fathers is that the Church is a "Hospital" which cures the wounded man. In many passages of Holy Scripture such language is used. One such passage is that of the parable of the Good Samaritan. "But a certain Samaritan, as he journeyed, came where he was: and when he saw him, he had compassion on him, And went to him, and bound up his wounds, pouring in oil and wine, and set him on his own beast, and brought him to an inn, and took care of him. And on the morrow when he departed, he took out two pence, and gave them to the host, and said unto him, Take care of him; and whatsoever thou spendest more, when I come again, I will repay thee" (Luk. 10, 33-35).

In this parable, the Samaritan represents Christ who cured the wounded man and led him to the Inn, that is to the "Hospital" which is the Church. It is evident here that Christ is presented as the Healer, the physician who cures man's maladies; and the Church as the true Hospital.

It is very characteristic that Saint Chrysostom, analysing this parable presents these truths emphasized above.

Man's life "in Paradise" was reduced to a life governed by the devil and his wiles. "And fell among thieves", that is in the hands of the devil and of all the hostile powers. The wounds man suffered are the various sins, as prophet David says: "my wounds grow foul and fester because of my foolishness" (Ps. 37). For "every sin causes a bruise and a wound". The Samaritan is Christ Himself who descended to earth from Heaven in order to cure the wounded man. He used oil and wine to "treat" the wounds; in other words by "mingling his blood with the Holy Spirit, he brought man to life". According to another interpretation, oil corresponds to the comforting word and wine to the harsh word. Mingled together they have the power to unify the scattered mind. "He set him in His own beast", that is He assumed human flesh on "the shoulders" of His Divinity and ascended incarnate to His Father in Heaven. Then the Good Samaritan, i.e. Christ, took man to the grand, wonderous and spacious inn -to the Church. And he handed man over to the inn-keeper, who is the Apostle Paul, and through the Apostle Paul to all bishops and priests, saying: "take care of the Gentile people, whom I have handed over to you in the Church. They suffer illness wounded by sin, so cure them, using as remedies the words of the Prophets and the teaching of the Gospel; make them healthy through the admonitions and comforting word of the Old and New Testaments".

Thus, according to St. Chrysostom, Paul is he who maintains the Churches of God, "curing all people by his spiritual admonitions and offering to each one of them what they really need"[4].

In the interpretation of this parable by St. Chrysostom it is clearly shown that the Church is a Hospital which cures people wounded by sin; and the bishops – priests are the therapists of the people of God.

---

4. See PG 62, 755-757

And this precisely is the work of Orthodox theology. When referring to Orthodox theology, we do not simply mean a history of theology. The latter is, of course, a part of this but not absolutely or exclusively. In patristic tradition, theologians are the God-seers. St. Gregory Palamas calls Barlaam a theologian, but he clearly emphasizes that intellectual theology differs greatly from the experience of the vision of God. According to St. Gregory Palamas theologians are the God-seers; those who have followed the "method" of the Church and have attained to perfect faith, to the illumination of the nous and to divinization (theosis). Theology is the fruit of man's cure and the path which leads to cure and the acquisition of the knowledge of God.

Western theology however has differentiated itself from Eastern Orthodox theology. Instead of being therapeutic, it is more intellectual and emotional in character. In the West, Scholastic theology evolved, which is antithetical to the Orthodox tradition. Western theology is based on rational thought whereas Orthodoxy is hesychastic. Scholastic theology tried to understand logically the Revelation of God and conform to philosophical methodology. Characteristic of such an approach is the saying of Anselm of Canterbury: "I believe so as to understand". The Scholastics acknowledged God at the outset and then endeavoured to prove His existence by logical arguments and rational categories. In the Orthodox Church, as expressed by the Holy Fathers, faith is God revealing Himself to man. We accept faith by hearing it not so that we can understand it rationally, but so that we can cleanse our hearts, attain to faith by "theoria"* and experience the Revelation of God.

Scholastic theology reached its culminating point in the person of Thomas Aquinas, a saint in the Roman-Catholic Church. He claimed that Christian truths are divided into natural and supernatural. Natural truths can be proven philosophically, like the truth of the Existence of God. Supernatural truths –such as the Triune God, the incarnation of the Logos, the resurrection of the bodies– cannot be proven philosophically, yet they cannot be disproven. Scholasticism linked theology very closely with philosophy, even more so with metaphysics. As a result, faith was altered and scholastic theology itself fell into complete disrepute when the "idol" of the West–metaphysics–collapsed. Scholasticism is held accountable for much of the tragic situation created in the West with respect to faith and faith issues.

The Holy Fathers teach that natural and metaphysical categories do not exist but speak rather of the created and uncreated. Never did the Holy Fathers accept Aristotle's metaphysics. However, it is not my intent to expound further on this. Theologians of the West during the Middle Ages considered scholastic theology to be a further development of the theology

---

*Theoria: Theoria is the vision of the glory of God. Theoria is identified with the vision of the uncreated Light, the uncreated energy of God, with the union of man with God, with man's theosis. Thus, theoria, vision and theosis are closely connected. Theoria has various degrees. There is illumination, vision of God and constant vision (for hours, days, weeks, even months). Noetic prayer is the first stage of theoria. Theoretical man is one who is at this stage. In patristic theology the theoretical man is characterised as the shepherd of the sheep.

of the Holy Fathers, and from this point on, begins the teaching of the Francs that scholastic theology is superior to that of the Holy Fathers. Consequently, Scholastics, who are occupied with reason, consider themselves superior to the Holy Fathers of the Church. They also believe that human knowledge, an offspring of reason, is loftier than Revelation and experience.

It is within this context that the conflict between St. Gregory Palamas and Barlaam should be viewed. Barlaam was essentially a scholastic theologian who attempted to pass on scholastic theology to the Orthodox East.

His views –that we cannot really know Who the Holy Spirit is exactly, (an outgrowth of which is agnosticism), that the ancient Greek philosophers are superior to the Prophets and the Apostles (since reason is above the vision of the Apostles), that the light of the Transfiguration is something which is created and can be undone, that the hesychastic way of life is not essential –i.e. the purification of the heart and the unceasing noetic prayer– are views which express a scholastic and subsequently, a secularized point of view of theology. St. Gregory Palamas foresaw the danger that these views held for Orthodoxy and through the power and energy of the Most Holy Spirit and the experience which he himself had acquired as successor to the Holy Fathers, he confronted this great danger and preserved unadulterated the Orthodox faith and tradition[5].

---

5. See Gregory Palamas, In Defence of the Holy Hesychasts, ed. Christou vol. I (Thessaloniki, 1962)

Having given a framework to the topic at hand, if Orthodox spirituality is examined in relationship to Roman-Catholicism and Protestantism the differences are immediately discovered.

Protestants do not have a "therapeutic treatment"-tradition. They suppose that believing in God, intellectually, constitutes salvation. Yet salvation is not a matter of intellectual acceptance of truth; rather it is a person's transformation and divinization by grace. This transformation is effected by the analogous "treatment" of one's personality, as shall be seen in the following chapters. In the Holy Scripture it appears that faith comes by hearing the Word and by experiencing "theoria" (the vision of God). We accept faith at first by hearing in order to be healed, and then we attain to faith by theoria, which saves man. Protestants because they believe that the acceptance of the truths of faith, the theoretical acceptance of God's Revelation, i.e. faith by hearing, saves man, do not have a "therapeutic tradition". It could be said that such a conception of salvation is very naive.

The Roman-Catholics as well do not have the perfection of the therapeutic tradition which the Orthodox Church has. Their doctrine of the filioque is a manifestation of the weakness in their theology to grasp the relationship existing between the person and society. They confuse the personal properties: the "unbegotten" of the Father, the "begotten" of the Son and the procession of the Holy Spirit. The Father is the cause of the "generation" of the Son and the procession of the Holy Spirit.

The Latins' weakness to comprehend and failure

to express the dogma of the Trinity shows the non-existence of empirical theology. The three disciples of Christ (Peter, James and John) beheld the glory of Christ on Mount Tabor; they heard at once the voice of the Father: "this is my beloved Son" and saw the coming of the Holy Spirit in a cloud –for, the cloud is the presence of the Holy Spirit, as St. Gregory Palamas says. Thus the disciples of Christ acquired the knowledge of the Triune God in theoria (vision of God) and by revelation. It was revealed to them that God is one essence in three hypostases.

This is what St. Symeon the New Theologian teaches. In his poems he proclaims over and over that while beholding the uncreated Light, the deified man acquires the Revelation of God the Trinity. Being in "theoria" (vision of God), the Saints do not confuse the hypostatic attributes. The fact that the Latin tradition came to the point of confusing these hypostatic attributes and teach that the Holy Spirit proceeds from the Son also, shows the non-existence of empirical theology for them. Latin tradition speaks also of created grace, a fact which suggests that there is no experience of the grace of God. For, when man obtains the experience of God, then he comes to understand well that this grace is uncreated. Without this experience there can be no genuine "therapeutic tradition".

And indeed we cannot find in all of Latin tradition, the equivalent to Orthodoxy's therapeutic method. The nous is not spoken of; neither is it distinguished from reason. The darkened nous is not treated as a malady and the illumination of the nous as therapy.

Many greatly publicized Latin texts are sentimental and exhaust themselves in a barren ethicology. In the Orthodox Church, on the contrary, there is a great tradition concerning these issues, which shows that within it there exists the true therapeutic method.

A faith is a true faith inasmuch as it has therapeutic benefits. If it is able to cure, then it is a true faith. If it does not cure, it is not a true faith. The same thing can be said about Medicine: A true scientist is the doctor who knows how to cure and his method has therapeutic benefits, whereas a charlatan is unable to cure. The same holds true where matters of the soul are concerned. The difference between Orthodoxy and the Latin tradition, as well as the Protestant confessions is apparent primarily in the method of therapy. This difference is made manifest in the doctrines of each denomination. Dogmas are not philosophy, neither is theology the same as philosophy.

Since Orthodox spirituality differs distinctly from the "spiritualities" of other confessions so much the more does it differ from the "spirituality" of Eastern religions, which do not believe in the Theanthropic nature of Christ and the Holy Trinity. They are influenced by the philosophical dialectic, which in Orthodox theology has been surpassed by the Revelation of God. These traditions are unaware of the notion of personhood and thus the hyposta tic principle. And love, as a fundamental teaching is totally absent. One may find, of course, in these Eastern religions an effort on the part of their followers to divest themselves of images and rational tho ughts, but this is in fact a movement towards nothingness, to non-existence. There is no

path leading their "disciples" to theosis–divinization*
of the whole man. There are many elements of
demonic "spirituality" in Eastern religions.

This is why a vast and chaotic gap exists between
Orthodox spirituality and the Eastern religions, in
spite of certain external similarities in terminology.
For example, Eastern religions may employ terms like
ecstasy , dispassion, illumination, noetic energy etc.
but they are impregnated with a content different
from corresponding terms in Orthodox spirituality.

---

*Theosis - Divinization: It is the participation in the uncreated grace
of God. Theosis is identified and connected with the theoria (vision)
of the uncreated Light. It is called theosis in grace because it is
attained through the energy, of the divine grace. It is a cooperation
of God with man, since God is He Who operates and man is he who
cooperates.

3. The Core of Orthodox Spirituality

In the Holy tradition of the Orthodox Church at the centre of Orthodox spirituality is the heart and the nous. It is this centre which needs to be treated so that man's complete psychosomatic constitution is cured. Moreover as the Lord said: "Blessed are the pure in heart: for they shall see God" (Matt. 5, 8). In order to see what the heart and nous are we must begin by examining the soul.

From the narration of Genesis in the Old Testament, we know that initially God created Adam's body and then He breathed into it and created his soul. By saying "He created the soul" it is made clear that the soul is not a particle of God, the spirit of God, as some people claim. But, as St. Chrysostom says, since the inbreathing of God is the energy of the Holy Spirit, it is this energy of the Holy Spirit which created the soul, without itself being the soul. It is of vital importance to state this, for thus we understand well that the soul cannot be examined autonomously but only in connection with God.

Every man's soul is one and manifold at the same time, as St. Gregory Palamas says. In another context St. Gregory Palamas teaches that as God is Trinity –Nous, Logos and Spirit– in a corresponding way man's soul has a trinitarian nature: there is the nous –the core of man's existence–, the logos –begotten by the nous– and the spirit –"man's noetic love".

The soul is closely linked to man's body. It is not located in only one part of the body.

According to Orthodox teaching God governs the world through his uncreated energies. Just as God acts in nature, so the soul moves and activates each member of the body to perform its function, according to St. Gregory of Sinai. Therefore, just as God governs the world in the same way does the soul govern the body.

As St. Gregory Palamas expresses it, the soul occupies the body with which it was created. It fills the entire body, giving life to the body. In other words, the soul is not enclosed by the body, but it occupies the body to which it is attached.

There is a strong bond between the soul and the body but also a clear distinction. A person is made up of body and soul, both of which coexist simultaneously without any confusion. Thus, it is not just the soul which is called man, neither is it solely the body which is called man, but both of them constitute man. The soul gives life to the whole body of man through its providential powers. However if the human body lacks one of its members, for example if a man has no eyes, this does not mean that the soul's providential powers are of a lesser degree. Moreover the soul is not in and of itself equivalent to her providential powers but she uniquely encloses all the providential. powers of the body[6].

St. Gregory of Nyssa states characteristically that the soul is not held by the body but it is she who contains the body. In other words, the body does not function as a vessel or a wine-skin, containing the soul,

---

6. See The Philokalia, ed. Astir vol. 4, Athens 1976, p. 156, § ξα΄

but rather the body is within her. The soul acts throughout the whole of man's body[7].

What has been said about the soul may seem highly theoretical, although it is a distinct teaching of the Church, and as such indispensable to the reader's understanding of the matter of heart and nous, which is the centre of Orthodox spirituality. We are not able, otherwise, to comprehend where the Orthodox Church is headed and what she seeks to cure.

As God has essence and energy, so also does the soul –having been made in the image of God– have essence and energy. Essence and energy in God are of course uncreated, whereas the soul's essence and energy are created. Nothing exists without an energy. The sun's essence is beyond the atmosphere of the earth, yet its energy, which gives light, heat and causes burning etc., reaches to earth and affords her with light, heat etc. The same happens with all objects. The soul's essence is found in the heart not like in a vessel but as if in an organ; its energy operates through the thoughts (logismoi).

According to St. Gregory Palamas, the soul is called the nous as well. Yet, both the essence of the soul –the heart– and its energy –consisting of the thoughts– are called nous[8].

However, although in the Biblical–Patristic tradition the terms are interchangeable, to avoid any confusion the soul is referred to as the spiritual element of man's existence; the heart, as the essence of the soul, and the nous, as the energy of the soul. Thus,

---

7. See PG 45, 217 β
8. See The Philokalia, ed. Astir vol. 4, Athens 1976, p. 133, § γ΄

when the nous enters the heart and acts therein, there exists a unity between the nous (energy), the heart (essence) and the soul[9].

All asceticism in the Church aims at man's theosis (divinization), at his communion with God the Trinity. This is accomplished when the energy of the soul (nous) returns to its essence (heart) and ascends to God. For unity with God to be attained, the unity of the soul, through the grace of God, must precede it. Sin in fact is the dispersion of these powers; it is primarily the scattering of the soul's energy, i.e. of the nous, to things and its separation from the heart.

Having made these clarifications it is important to examine more analytically what the heart and nous are in Orthodox tradition.

The heart is the centre of man's psychosomatic constitution, since, as we noted previously, there is an "unconfused" union between soul and body. The centre of this union is called heart.

The heart is the place which is discovered through ascetic practice in a state of grace; it is the place wherein God is revealed and made manifest. This definition may seem abstract, yet it is a matter of spiritual experience. Noone can fully show the place of the heart by rational and speculative definitions. In any case the heart is the centre and summation of the three faculties of the soul: of the intellect, the appetitive and the irascible. The fact is that when a person lives the inner life –when his nous returns within his inner world from its previous dispersion; when he experiences mourning and, in the deepest sense,

9. See The Philokalia, ed. Astir vol. 4, Athens 1976, p. 132, § β´

repentance– he is then conscious of the existence of this centre, i.e. the existence of the heart. He feels therein pain and spiritual sorrow; he experiences the grace of God; there also he even hears the voice of God.

According to patristic tradition, the essence of the soul, which is called heart, is found as if within an organ, not in a vessel where the physical organ of the heart is. This should be interpreted in reference to what it was said before, that the soul holds the body and gives life to it; it is not contained by the body but it contains the person's body. It is within this perspective that St. Nicodemos the Hagiorite speaks of the heart as a biophysical (natural) centre, since the blood is circulated to all parts of the body from there; as an affected (contrary to nature) centre, since the passions prevail therein, and as a supernatural centre since the grace of God operates there, as many passages of the Holy Scripture state:

"But I say unto you, That whosoever looketh on a woman to lust after her hath committed adultery with her already in his heart" (Matt. 5, 28)

"But after thy hardness and impenitent heart treasurest up unto thyself wrath against the day of wrath and revelation of the righteous judgement of God" (Rom. 2, 5)

"That Christ may dwell in your hearts by faith" (Eph. 3, 17)

"And hope maketh not ashamed; because the love of God is shed abroad in our hearts by the Holy Ghost which is given unto us" (Rom. 5, 5)

The nous, on the other hand, is the energy of the soul. According to the Fathers, the nous is also called the eye of the soul. Its natural place is to be found within the heart; to be united with the essence of the soul and to experience the unceasing memory of God. Its movement goes contrary to nature when it is enslaved by the creatures of God and the passions. Orthodox tradition makes a distinction between nous and reason.

Reason is a function in the brain whereas the nous operates out of and is united with the heart in its natural state. In the saintly person, who is the manifestation and bearer of Orthodox spirituality, reason works and is conscious of the surrounding world while the nous is within the heart, praying unceasingly. The separation of the nous from reason constitutes the state of a spiritually healthy person, and this is the goal of Orthodox spirituality.

Quite illustrative of the above theme are two passages from St. Basil the Great's writings. In one text he says that in the spiritual man –who has become a temple of God and of the Most Holy Spirit– reason and the nous exist and operate simultaneously. Reason is engaged in earthly cares and the nous is engaged in the unceasing remembrance of God. Moreover, because his nous is united with the heart and has communion with God, man is not disturbed by unexpected temptations, that is to say, by temptations caused by the decay and transiency of his nature[10].

In the other passage St. Basil refers to the return of the nous into the heart and its ascent to God.

----

10. See St. Basil the Great, Greek Fathers of the Church (in Greek, E.Π.E.), Thessaloniki 1972, Vol. 1, p. 68

The latter passage should be interpreted within the context of the former one and in relationship to all of St. Basil's teaching. The nous which is scattered outwards and diffused through the senses into the world is sick, fallen, prodigal. It must return from its diffused state to its union with and in the heart, its natural state, and then be united with God. Illumined by the uncreated Light (the state of theosis), the nous neglects even its nature, and the soul is not preoccupied with clothing and shelter. This does not mean that man does not care about food, etc. But, because man has attained to the state of theoria (vision of God) and theosis, his bodily forces –not those of the soul– are in a state of suspension; in other words, the soul and nous are not subjugated by the influences of the world and material things. Man is, of course, concerned about them, yet he is not enslaved by them. Additionally, St. Basil the Great clearly states that by this movement of the nous' return within the heart, virtue as a whole is acquired: prudence, bravery, justice, wisdom along with all of the other virtues[11].

Fr. John Romanides[12] says that all living creatures possess two known memory-systems. First, "there is the cell memory which determines the development and growth of the individual in relationship to itself". This is the known D.N.A. structure which is the genetic code that literally defines everything in the human constitution. Secondly, "there is the brain cell

---

11. See St. Basil the Great, Greek Fathers of the Church (in Greek, E.Π.E.), Thessaloniki 1972, Vol. 1, pp. 64-66
12. See John Romanides, "Franks, Romans Feudalism and Doctrine" Holy Cross Orthodox Press, 1981

memory which determines the functions and relations of the individual towards himself and his environment". This is the operation of the brain which –being imprinted by all memories of the past as well as by human knowledge acquired through study and investigation– defines man's relations with his fellow-human beings. In addition though, according to Romanides, "there exists within every person a mal-functioning or sub-functioning memory within the heart; and when activated through noetic prayer it has perpetual memory of God, which contributes to the normalization of all of a person's other relations.

Consequently the Saint –a bearer of Orthodox spirituality– possesses all three of these memories, which act and function simultaneously without influencing one another. A Saint is the most "natural of men". He is conscious of the world, involved in various concerns, yet –because his nous has attained to its natural function– "he lives on earth but is a citizen of heaven".

Therefore, the centre of Orthodox spirituality is the heart, within which man's nous must inherently operate. The energy of the soul –the nous– must return within the soul's essence –in the heart–; and thus by uniting these powers by the grace of God acquire unity and communion with God the Trinity. A spirituality outside of this perspective is not Orthodox but moralistic, pietistic, abstract and rationalistic.

4. Degrees of Spiritual Perfection

In the preceding chapters it was revealed that the most important work of the Church is to cure man. Therefore the Orthodox Church is a Hospital, an infirmary of the soul. This does not mean that the Church disregards other domains of pastoral activity, since she aims at the whole of man, consisting of both body and soul. She cares indeed for the physical, economic and social problems as well; yet the main weight of her pastoral service is put on the soul's therapy, for when man's soul is cured then many other intractable problems are solved.

Some people accuse the Orthodox Church of not being very much involved in social problems. However the Church does care about all matters which concern man. This is evident in the content of her prayers during the worship services as well as in the work and teaching of the Holy Fathers. But just as a medical Hospital is primarily interested in the treatment of the body –and through this therapy it gets involved with the rest of a person's problems– so it is in the Orthodox Church. She cures the core of human personality and through this, she heals the whole person. That is why even during times of social upheavals, when all governmental mechanisms are virtually brought to a halt –even peoples' external freedoms are disrupted– the Church maintains its work: to treat and cure the person.

Healing of man's personality is in fact his progress toward perfection which is actually identified with "theosis", for in patristic theology theosis and perfection are synonymous terms. And this therapy is absolutely necessary, because man's fall, effected in the person of Adam, constitutes the sickness of man's nature.

In Paradise, before the Fall, Adam was in the state of "theoria" (vision) of God. The study of the book of Genesis reveals that Adam was in communion with God; however it was necessary for him to remain in that state, by virtue of his voluntary struggle, in order for him to become more stabilized and reach perfect communion and union with Him. St. John of Damascus describes this state of primordial "justice" characteristically. Adam was purified and nourished at the same time by the vision of God. His nous was illumined, and this signifies above all that he was a temple of the Holy Spirit, and was experiencing unceasing remembrance of God.

"Original" sin consists in the darkening of the nous and the loss of communion with God. This, of course, had other repercussions, as well: man was clothed in the fleshly garments of decay and mortality. The nous experienced a deep darkness. In other words, man lost the illumination of his nous; it became impure, impassioned and his body bore corruption and mortality. Thus, from the day of our birth, we bear within us corruption and death: a human life is brought into the world bound for death. Hence, because of the fall we experience universal malady. Both soul and body are sick and naturally, since man is the summation of all creation, –the microcosmos within the megacosmos– corruption also befell all of creation.

"My mind is wounded, my body has grown feeble, my spirit is sick, my speech has lost its power, my life is dead; the end is at the door. What shalt thou do, then, miserable soul, when the Judge comes to examine thy deeds?" (Great Canon).

In fact, when we speak of original sin and its consequences, we mean three things: first, the malfunction of the nous, since the nous ceased to work properly; secondly, the identification of the nous with reason (and to a certain extent, the deification of reason) and thirdly the nous' enslavement to the passions, anxiety and the conditions of the environment. And this constitutes man's real death.

He experiences total disorganization; his inner self is deadened –his nous is overcome by darkness. And just as when the eye of the body is hurt, the whole body is obscure, so also when the eye of the soul –the nous– suffers blindness, the spiritual self as a whole becomes sick. It falls into deepest darkness. This is what the Lord is referring, when He says: "If therefore the light that is in thee be darkness, how great is that darkness!" (Matt. 6, 23).

In addition to the disruption of the soul's entire inner workings, original sin resulted also in the disorganization of man outwardly. He now confronts his fellow-men, God, the world and all of creation in a different way. The nous is unable to encounter God; so reason undertakes the effort. Thus idols of God are created leading to pagan religions and even heretical deviations.

Incapable of seeing man as an image of God, the nous encounters him under the influence of the passions. He ambitiously exploits his fellow-man, through his love of pleasure and material gain. He regards him as a vessel or instrument of pleasure; at the same time he idolizes all of creation, which is what the Apostle Paul describes in his Epistle to the Romans: "Professing themselves to be wise, they became fools, And changed the glory of the uncorruptible God into an image made like to corruptible man, and to birds, and fourfooted beasts, and creeping things" (Rom. 1, 22-23).

Therefore man needs to be cured, that is to be purified, to reach the illumination of the nous – Adam's state before the Fall– and then attain theosis. This is achieved precisely through Christ's incarnation and the entire work of Divine Economy and of the Church. It is within this frame of reference we must see many liturgical texts according to which Christ is characterised as physician and healer of souls and bodies. Moreover, in the same framework various patristic texts should be studied, where it is apparent that the work of Christ is first and foremost a therapeutic one.

The heretic Apollinarios claimed that by his incarnation Christ assumed soul and body but not nous. He said, in other words, that the human nature which Christ assumed from the Panagia, was deprived of nous. Refuting his heresy, St. Gregory the Theologian stated that Christ assumed the whole of man; for, what is not assumed cannot be cured, whereas what is united with God is saved. If half of Adam sinned, then this would be assumed by God to be saved. Yet, since the whole of Adam sinned and the totality of human nature fell into sickness, the whole person had to be fully assumed by Christ so as to be healed. In St. Gregory's teaching of this it is evident that the cure of human nature was realized by the Incarnation of the Son and Logos of God; and this is why Christ is the true therapist and physician of man[13].

After the Fall man needed cure. This was effected by the Incarnation of Christ and ever since then this has been the work of the Church. She cures and is curing man; she primarily cures his ailing personality –his nous and heart. All the Fathers of the Church exhort man to seek to be cured[14]. Man is cured by the energy of God whose source is uncreated and revealed "in the person of Jesus Christ". Christ's energy, from which comes man's cure, is granted freely, and for this reason is called divine grace. Therefore, whether we say uncreated energy or divine grace makes no difference; we mean the same thing. The Apostle Paul writes: "For by grace are ye saved through faith; and that not of yourselves: it is the gift of God" (Eph. 2, 8).

Living within the Church by grace, man must first cleanse his heart of the passions; attain the illumination of the nous –Adam's state before the Fall– and then ascend to theosis, which constitutes man's communion and union with God and is identified with salvation. These are the steps of spiritual perfection –the foundations of Orthodox spirituality.

Yet a few things about the divine grace need to be said before we see the stages of spiritual perfection –the method and way of man's therapy– for it is closely connected with purification, illumination and theosis.

---

13. See St. Gregory the Theologican, Greek Fathers of the Church (in Greek, E.Π.E.), Thessaloniki 1986, Vol. 7, p. 182
14. See Ibid, Vol. 5, p. 316

In Orthodox spirituality purification, illumination and theosis are not stages of anthropocentric activity, but rather they are results of the uncreated energy of God. When the divine grace (energy of God) purifies man from passions, it is called purifying; when it illumines his nous it is called illuminating; and when it deifies man it is called deifying. This same grace and energy of God is given various names according to its effects.

Talking about the Triune God, the Holy Fathers say that there are in God essence or nature, energy or divine grace, and the persons. Each Person of the Holy Trinity has essence and personal attributes. The personal attributes pertain to each Person. Essence is common in the three Persons as is energy. Creation and recreation of man and the world is the common action of God the Trinity. Man's salvation is an energy of the Trinity God, yet "in the person of Jesus Christ", since Christ was incarnate "by condescension of the Father and the synergy of the Holy Spirit".

It must be noted that God's energies are "natural", they are linked, that is, with God's nature; yet at the same time, they are hypostatic. In order to grasp this concept one should refer to the teaching of St. John of Damascus, where he states that energy is the potent and essential activity of nature. It is another thing the nature from which energy derives (ενεργητικόν–energetikon); and the hypostasis who makes use of the energy, whereby one acts (ενεργών–energon) as well as the effect of the energy (ενέργημα–energima)[15].

---

15. St. John of Damascus, "The complete presentation of the Orthodox faith" (in Greek), ed. Pournaras, p. 272

This means that divine energy is the activity of divine nature through which man participates in and is united with God. There is no essence without energy, neither is there energy without essence. Yet, this divine energy is revealed in man and by his participation in the hypostasis, since he who acts is the hypostasis, the person. Thus, the energy of God is natural and not self-existent. Although it is not self-existent it is enhypostatic, in other words, it acts upon and is participated in by man through the hypostasis. Thus, we know God, come into communion with Him and participate in His uncreated grace and energy through the Revelation and Incarnation of Christ.

We said before that uncreated energy, divine grace, according to its effects, has various names. For example, there is the purifying, there is the illuminating and also the deifying energy of God. For this reason three stages of spiritual perfection can be distinguished: purification of the heart, illumination of the nous and thirdly theosis. Just as a person must successfully pass through elementary, intermediate and higher levels of education in order to attain to knowledge, so also he must go through three stages of spiritual perfection –purification of heart, illumination of nous and theosis– so as to acquire divine knowledge. In this manner a person is cured.

Two points must be emphasized before moving on to an analysis of these three stages of spiritual perfection, in order to avoid misunderstanding this teaching of the Church Fathers:

The first point is that attaining to these stages is not the result of human effort but rather of the energy of God. They are not measures, that is, that involve the positive exercising of a person's will; they are the fruits and outcome–actions of the uncreated grace of God. These stages of spiritual perfection naturally develop in those people who co-operate and respond to the energy of divine grace.

The second point is that the distinction made among these spiritual stages is neither static nor air-tight. In public education when one finishes elementary school, he is not going back again. This does not hold true in "theanthropic pedagogy", which we undergo within the Church, because the three stages of spiritual growth are interchangeable. In order for the person to attain to the "theoria" of God, purification and illumination must precede. When he attains to the theoria of God –the third stage of spiritual perfection– he may remain there for a certain period of time and then again he may "go back" to the state of illumination of the nous. Also, if he is not careful, it is possible for him to lapse from the illumination of the nous to the stage of purification.

Throughout all patristic tradition the Fathers allude to the three stages of spiritual perfection as the three degrees of one's cure. St. Dionysios the Areopagite makes mention of purification, illumination and perfection. St. Gregory of Nyssa also makes use of the same distinction. St. Maximos the Confessor refers, as well, to practical philosophy (purification), natural theoria (illumination) and mystical theology (theosis). St. Symeon the New Theologian, in his writings divides certain chapters into practical, gnostic and theological. In all of Orthodox Tradition these three stages of perfection are frequently mentioned. In this way man is cured and experiences Holy Tradition; he becomes "Tradition" and creates Tradition. He is a bearer of Tradition. Distinctive is the subtitle of Philokalia which is the work of St. Nicodemos, of the Holy Mountain and of St. Makarios, Bishop of Corinth. In this work which is a compilation of the writings of the holy Fathers, how man cures his nous by going through the three stages of spiritual life is discussed. And it is known that the Philokalia, which contains the complete method of cure for humans is a fundamental manual of the spiritual life[16].

In order for this teaching of the Church Fathers to become more comprehensible, the author would like to refer more extensively here to the teaching of St. Niketas Stethatos, where the three stages of spiritual life are analysed. St. Niketas is a bearer of Holy Tradition; he is integrally placed within the entire traditional teaching of cure in the Orthodox Church.

He writes that a person must necessarily pass through the three categories of ascent, so as to participate in and attain to the "fullness" of Christ, and to achieve, in effect, his salvation. These three stages correspond to beginners, intermediate and perfected Christians.

St. Niketas Stethatos speaks repeatedly in his works of this ascent. He continually talks about the three classes and degrees of the spiritual life, since we must direct ourselves progressively toward God and not remain static. From ascetic practice we must ascend to the natural theoria of creation and move on to mystical theology of logos. Moreover he claims that if we do not experience this state and do not strive for

---

16. See The Philokalia, ed. Astir, Athens 1976

perfection, we are worse than the people of the world who are constantly pursuing positions of status[17].

This ascent is not independent of the purification stage and that of illumination. Man should first be purified from his enslavement to creatures. He then acquires illumined and radiant noetic eyes. This is achieved through mystical wisdom, hidden in God; In this manner he will ascend to the science of sacred knowledge. Only then does man become a theologian and impart the mystical concepts of divine wisdom to the receptive ones.

Apart from this general outline given concerning the three categories of the faithful and the three stages of spiritual perfection St. Niketas offers an extensive description of the atmosphere surrounding the stages of spiritual life[18].

The stage of purification (that of the beginners) in the "warfare" for godliness is closely linked with repentance. By repentance we mean, on the one hand the discarding of the old, earthly man, and on the other hand, the "putting on" of the new man, who is restored by the energy of the Most Holy Spirit.

Thus, repentance, which is experienced at the stage of purification is made manifest by a feeling of contempt towards matter (essentially, it is contempt for the passions connected with matter); by the "melting" of the flesh through fasting and vigilance; by staying away from any cause which incites passion; by the shedding of tears; by penitence for the past; by adjusting one's actions to the integrity of the spirit; by

---

cleansing the nous from any defilement, through holy
compunction; and by the advent of the Logos into the
nous.

In general it is in following the ascetic life that
repentance finds expression. By repenting man extin-
guishes the strength of inborn fire; he silences the
mouths of reckless passions –he becomes spiritually
strong.

The stage of illumination constitutes the first dispassion[19]. A characteristic trait of this level is the
knowledge of beings; the "theoria" of the causes of
beings and the participation in the Holy Spirit. The
benefits of illumination are the purification of nous by
the divine grace, which consumes the heart like fire;
the noetic revelation of the "eye of the heart" and the
birth of the Word within the nous, expressed in noble
sense. In other words, in this state man acquires
knowledge of God and unceasing noetic prayer.
Moreover, man comes to know things human and
divine and experiences the revelation of the mysteries
of the kingdom of Heaven.

The mystical and perfecting stage is that of the
perfected ones, who, in fact become the theologians
of the Church. The deified man then comes into co n-
munion with the angelic powers; he approaches the
uncreated Light; the depths of God are revealed to
him through the Holy Spirit, and thus he beholds the
uncreated essential energy of God. This man comes to
know many mysteries existing in the Holy Scripture as
well, yet hidden from other people. He ascends to the
"third heaven" of theology, like Apostle Paul, and

---

19. See The Philokalia, ed. Astir 1976, vol. 3, p. 331, § κβ´

hears ineffable words and sees what corporal man's eyes cannot see. He becomes a theologian within the Church and experiences the blessed state of "rest in God".

There are those of course who claim that defining the stages of spiritual life is an influence of ancient Greek philosophy, especially of neoplatonism, wherein discourse on asceticism and knowledge of the Divine was a common place. However if we examine things carefully we realise that in ancient Greece the philosophers talked about purification and illumination differently from how and what the Holy Fathers teach.

In Platonic philosophy, purification is the mortification of the appetitive and irascible power of the soul; the platonics believed that man is mainly his reason, whereas both the appetitive and irascible power are the result of the Fall. Thus, talking of purification the ancients primarily referred to the mortification of the soul's powers. Also for the ancient philosophers illumination was the knowledge of the archetypes of existence, since they believed that man forgot these archetypes after his Fall, and this constituted human tragedy and condemnation. However, in Orthodoxy purification, illumination and theosis have a different content and character.

We must say that in speaking of purification, illumination and theosis the holy Fathers were not influenced by ancient Greek philosophy or neoplatonism; they had the experience and lived this reality. And this experience of communion with God in a different way, of course, is encountered in both the Old and New Testaments. There are many passages in Holy Scripture indicating that for man's ascent to God purification of the heart from the passions must precede and then man acquires an illumined nous with constant remembrance of God.

Firstly we should examine Christ's teaching about the knowledge of the mysteries of the kingdom of God. After the sower's parable the disciples asked Him to explain the meaning of it to them. Then Christ said: "Unto you it is given to know the mysteries of the kingdom of God: but to others in parables; that seeing they might not see, and hearing they might not understand" (Luk. 8, 10).

Christ's response shows that there are people who hear the Word of God in parables, but they are not prepared to receive the mysteries of the Kingdom of God, because they have not been cleansed. There are others like the Disciples, who are worthy to receive the mysteries of the Kingdom of Heaven by virtue of their purification; i.e. their abandonment of all things of the world and following Christ. Add to this, the event of the three disciples who ascended Mount Tabor and beheld the Kingdom of God, and one arrives at the third category of Christians.

Thus throughout the centuries there are people who hear the word of God in parables; others who are worthy of seeing the mysteries of the kingdom of Heaven without beholding them yet; and still others worthy of the theoria of God –they see God Himself.

Moreover in Christ's sermon on the Mount, particularly in the Beatitudes, it is evident that man must first be purified from the passions, cleanse his heart from all thoughts dwelling within and acquire humility of spirit so as to become worthy of seeing God.

"Blessed are the poor in spirit: for theirs is the kingdom of heaven.

Blessed are they that mourn: for they shall be comforted.

Blessed are the meek: for they shall inherit the earth.

Blessed are they which do hunger and thirst after righteousness: for they shall be filled.

Blessed are the merciful: for they shall obtain mercy.

Blessed are the pure in heart: for they shall see God"

(Matt. 5, 3-8)

The Beatitudes show man's spiritual journey, the path of theosis; the way by which his cure is achieved. The awareness of his spiritual poverty –the recognition of the passions existing in his heart– leads man to repentance and blessed mourning. Analogous to the degree of his mourning there comes within his soul divine comfort –divine consolation. It is in this way that he obtains meekness and inner tranquillity. Experiencing meekness within makes him yet even more thirsty for the justice of God and the keeping of His commandments in everyday life. By upholding the commandments of God, man gains knowledge of God's mercy, and his heart is further cleansed. For this is the work of the commandments –the purification of the soul. Some of these commandments refer to the cleansing of the intelligible aspect of the soul; others to the appetitive power and others result in the purification and strengthening of the irascible power of the soul. Thus when the soul is purified from the passions, man reaches the theoria of God.

The Beatitudes manifest the essence of spiritual life and manner in which a person is cured. By keeping the commandments, man is sealed with the seal of the Most Holy Spirit and becomes a member of the Body of Christ; a temple of the Most Holy Spirit.

In the parable of the prodigal Son it is clear that there are three categories of saved men. The servants belong to the first category. (..."but the father said to his servants"). In the second category the hired servants are included. ("How many hired servants of my father's have bread enough and to spare"). Finally, the sons of the father belong to the third category ("A certain man had two sons"...). Thus the father in the parable had sons, hired servants and servants (Luke 15, 11-32).

In the teaching of the Holy Fathers one finds the view that the saved ones belong in three categories. Firstly, there are the servants who uphold the will of God, so as to avoid Hell; secondly, there are the "tenants" who follow the commandments in order to gain Paradise; and finally in the third category there are the sons who, out of their love for God, do everything just because they feel as His children. These three categories correspond in fact to the three stages of spiritual life: purification, illumination and theosis.

Apart from Christ's teaching on the purification of heart, illumination of nous and theosis and to which we referred earlier, there are many passages in the New Testament where the way toward salvation and theosis is spoken of. I would like to mention only a few from the Apostle Paul's teachings.

He speaks characteristically about purification of heart: "Having therefore these promises, dearly beloved, let us cleanse ourselves from all filthiness of the flesh and spirit, perfecting holiness in the fear of God" (2 Cor. 7, 1). Holiness is effected in the fear of God and especially by purification. It is only through the purification of the heart that we can participate in the sanctification, that is the deifying energy of God.

There are also many passages about the illumination of the nous manifested mainly in noetic prayer. In his 1st epistle to the Corinthians the Apostle Paul teaches that only when one has the Holy Spirit within him can he say "Jesus is the Lord". "Wherefore I give you to understand, that no man speaking by the Spirit of God calleth Jesus accursed: and that no man can say that Jesus is the Lord, but by the Holy Ghost" (1 Cor. 12, 3). What is implied here is not the worship of reason but the what is called noetic worship –the prayer which is activated within man's heart. For, in order for someone to pray "logically", the presence of the Most Holy Spirit is not necessary. Everybody can pray with his logic and say Jesus is the Lord. Yet the Apostle Paul says: "no man can say that Jesus is the Lord, but by the Holy Ghost". The word "no one" signifies that only in the Holy Spirit can a person have noetic prayer within his heart.

Placing this quotation within the framework of St. Paul's whole teaching, we shall see clearly it refers to the prayer of the heart which acts within the heart at the stage of illumination of the nous. To the Ephesians he writes: "...but be filled with the Spirit; Speaking to yourselves in psalms and hymns and spiritual songs, singing and making melody in your heart to the Lord" (Eph. 5, 18-19). The psalms, hymns and spiritual songs are said within the heart when man is filled with the Holy Spirit.

Noetic prayer is done within the heart, since man acquired sonship in the Holy Spirit. He became, that is, son of God by grace. Writes the Apostle to the Romans: "For as many as are led by the Spirit of God, they are the sons of God. For ye have not received the spirit of bondage again to fear; but ye have received the Spirit of adoption, whereby we cry, Abba, Father. The Spirit itself beareth witness with our spirit, that we are the children of God" (Rom. 8, 14-16).

Noetic prayer, operating within the heart in the Holy Spirit, is closely related to sonship by grace. This means that purification of heart precedes, whereby all thoughts–logismoi* are expelled from therein; then man becomes a son of God by grace and he prays naturally by saying "Abba father". It is then that he becomes a real member of the Church since, according to the divine Apostle again, "if any man have not the Spirit of Christ, he is none of his" (Rom. 8, 9).

The Apostle Paul calls this state illumination: the advent of divine grace into man's heart, after having purified and illumined it. "For God, who commanded the light to shine out of darkness, hath shined in our hearts, to give the light of the knowledge of the glory of God in the face of Jesus Christ" (2 Cor, 4, 6). Spiritual darkness is the benighted nous. The grace of God, coming in the face of Christ, shines in the heart

---

*Thoughts - Logismoi: The thoughts which are connected with images as well as with the various stimulations originating from the senses and the imagination. The thoughts–logismoi evolve to sin through the stages of *desire, action* and *passion*. They are called *logismoi* because they act in the reason (logiki, in Greek). It can be said that the term "fixations" conveys to a large extent the same meaning.

of the illumined and grants to him the light of the knowledge of the glory of God.

Many quotations can be presented referring to theosis and theoria of God. The Apostle Paul himself mentions quite frequently the Revelation he received from God: "It is not expedient for me doubtless to glory. I will come to visions and revelations of the Lord. I knew a man in Christ above fourteen years ago, (whether in the body, I cannot tell; or wether out of the body, I cannot tell; God knoweth;) such an one caught up to the third heaven. And I knew such a man, (whether in the body, or out of the body, I cannot tell: God knoweth;) How that he was caught up into paradise, and heard unspeakable words, which it is not lawful for a man to utter. Of such an one will I glory: yet of myself I will not glory, but in mine infirmities. For though I would desire to glory, I shall not be a fool; for I will say the truth: but now I forbear, lest any man should think of me above that which he seeth me to be, or that he heareth of me. And lest I should be exalted above measure through the abundance of the revelations, there was given to me a thorn in the flesh, the messenger of Satan to buffet me, lest I should be exalted above measure. For this thing I besought the Lord thrice, that it might depart from me. And he said unto me, My grace is sufficient for thee: for my strength is made perfect in weakness. Most gladly therefore will I rather glory in my infirmities, that the power of Christ may rest upon me" (2 Cor, 12, 1-9).

As we know from the holy tradition of our Church, theoria of God is attained through man's theosis and this is why man participates in the deifying energy of God.

Spiritual life, therefore, is not an anthropocentric condition but the experience of God's uncreated grace. It is not philosophy or speculation but participation in the grace of God. The Apostle Peter refers also to the vision of the glory of God on Mount Tabor.

"For we have not followed cunningly devised fables, when we made known unto you the power and coming of our Lord Jesus Christ, but were eyewitnesses of his majesty. For he received from God the Father honour and glory, when there came such a voice to him from the excellent glory, This is my beloved Son, in whom I am well pleased. And this voice which came from heaven we heard, when we were with him in the holy mount. We have also a more sure word of prophecy; whereunto ye do well that ye take heed, as unto a light that shineth in a dark place, until the day dawn, and the day star arise in your hearts: knowing this first, that no prophecy of the scripture is of any private interpretation. For the prophecy came not in old time by the will of man: but holy men of God spake as they were moved by the Holy Ghost" (2 Peter, 1, 16-21)

In the foregoing passage, apart from the fact that Christian Revelation is not speculation but experience of the living God, it is clear at the same time that man should uphold the prophetic word which is as a lamp shining his path, "until the day dawns and the morning star rises in your hearts".

In the New Testament, therefore, both in the words of Christ and the sayings of the Apostles the three stages of the spiritual life are indicated; the degrees of spiritual perfection and man's cure: the purification of heart, the illumination of the nous and theosis. This is indeed man's true way towards theosis. Adam in Paradise was in the state of illumination and vision of God. Yet he lost this glory after the sin he committed. In fact sin is the loss of the glory of God - of theoria. The Apostle Paul says: "For all have sinned, and come short of the glory of God; Being justified freely by his grace through the redemption that is in Christ Jesus" (Rom. 3, 23-24). Sin is connected with the loss of the glory of God, with the loss of theoria. And, naturally, man has the capacity to be justified, to reach to theoria and theosis through the incarnation of Christ. Thus, justification is theosis and man's salvation.

5. Praxis and Theoria

In the teachings of the Holy Fathers, the three stages of the spiritual life are characterized by use of the terms "praxis" and "theoria". I think we should dwell upon this subject also, in order, on the one hand to understand more clearly what is meant by repentance and purification of heart; and, on the other hand, to ascertain the misinterpretation of the terms "praxis" and "theoria" by contemporary individuals. I would like to begin with an analysis of the latter.

When reading texts from the Holy Fathers, many people behold these terms without being aware of their deeper meaning. They interpret them within the perspective of Western thought: "Theoria" is termed as speculative, is based on theory not on practice, in other words, dealing simply with logic theoretically. Whereas "praxis" is the teaching and application of these intellectual concepts. Still others see "theoria" as the reflection on things divine, and "praxis" as its missionary thrust, i.e. the teaching of these rational concepts.

However, in the Patristic tradition other meanings are attached to the terms "praxis" and "theoria", which shall be referred to briefly in the following passages.

St. Gregory the Theologian says that theoria and praxis are beneficial, because theoria elevates man's nous above earthly things; it guides him to the holy of holies and restores him to his original nature; whereas praxis receives and serves Christ and tests love with actions. Clearly, theoria is the vision of God –the nous' restoration and return to God; praxis is whatever deeds it takes to lead to this love[20].

In another text, St. Gregory the Theologian, in making reference to the last and the most dreadful of the seven plagues of the Egyptians –i.e. the death of their first-born children– states that in order for a person to escape the angel of death, he must anoint the guardians of his nous –praxis and theoria– with the blood of Christ. Thus praxis and theoria are linked with the nous. They are nous' guardians and are cured by the blood of Christ. And this, for certain, is our identification with and participation in Christ's crucifixion, burial, resurrection and ascension.

Within the whole of patristic tradition it is clear that praxis is the purification of the heart's passions and theoria is both the illumination of the nous and the vision of the uncreated glory of God. According to St. Gregory the Theologian, praxis is the cause of theoria. According to Elias the Elder, praxis is fasting and all night vigil; psalm-singing and prayer; and silence which is more precious than words; also praxis is whatever is done patiently without complaint. St. Isaac the Syrian says that theoria is the vision of the nous". It must be noted, of course, that there is no praxis independent of theoria, neither does theoria exist independently of praxis. This means that man is led to the theoria of God through purification; and when theoria ceases, then praxis begins again.

---

20. See St. Gregory the Theologian, Greek Fathers of the Church (in Greek, E.Π.E.), Thessaloniki 1977, Vol. 5, p. 246

St. Gregory Palamas is more analytical on the subject of praxis and theoria. He teaches that theoria of God is nothing else but the vision of God. Therefore theoria is not speculation on what is said or what is seen, but it is the vision of God. If this is in fact theoria, then it follows that praxis is nothing less than the cleansing of the heart, and repentance , the complete hesychastic way of life, instruction on hesychia. Thus, according to St. Gregory Palamas, praxis is equated with hesychasm, a method of prayer (holy silence) which necessitates stillness of the nous; the halting of the world, and the forgetting of earthly things. It is an initiation into the things from above and the putting aside of all concepts of goodness. Through praxis –sacred hesychia– "we are liberated from what is worldly and direct ourselves toward God". This is the path and manner of ascent towards God which the Most Holy Mother of God followed; she attained to theosis thus and became the mother of the Word of God[21].

Praxis, therefore, is the purification of the heart; this constitutes genuine repentance, as proclaimed by St. John the Baptist, Christ Himself and, of course, by all of His Apostles, because repentance is the indispensable prerequisite for one to experience the Kingdom of God.

Thus, purification of the heart, i.e. of our inner world, is the first stage of the spiritual life, through which we must pass in order to attain to salvation.

In the following the meaning attached to "purifica-

---

21. See St. Gregory Palamas, Greek Fathers of the Church (in Greek, Ε.Π.Ε.), Thessaloniki 1986, Vol. 11, p. 328

tion of heart" by the Holy Fathers must be ascertained. They intend primarily three things.

Firstly, purification of the heart is the cure of the soul's faculty, so as to function in accordance with nature and above nature –not contrary to nature. Man's soul is both unified and manifold. She has primarily three faculties: the intelligent, the appetitive and the incentive. All three faculties, when functioning normally, are directed towards God. The intellect seeks God; the desire longs for God, and the will must do everything to achieve this communion and union with God.

Secondly, purification is man's deliverance from pleasure and pain, in other words a person's liberation from the oppression exerted by pleasure and pain. When man is cleansed, he is freed from their domination. It is the spiritual pleasures which primarily are cultivated within him; and he does not become distressed or afflicted when diverse people or problems and adversities in life cause him pain.

Thirdly, purification is the cleansing of the heart from the various thoughts-logismoi* existing therein. They are called logismoi because they must dwell in the reason and not within the heart. What does this mean? When a "logismos" comes and a person is not sufficiently attentive, it then becomes a desire which wants to be fulfilled, i.e. realized. This means that the logismos proceeds from the intelligent faculty of the soul to the passible faculty, that is the faculties of the appetitive and the incentive. Being realized and developing into a passion the logismos enters, in fact, into the heart and remains all powerful there.

---

*See Footnote p. 56

The Fathers say that the heart can be cleansed of logismoi through repentance and by means of the ascetic method of the Church. And this ascetic method is inspired by divine grace. A simple thought may enter the reason but not find its way within the heart. When all logismoi are dismissed and the heart is cleansed, only one word-prayer prevails. For this reason the prayer "Lord Jesus Christ , have mercy on me" is called the one-word-prayer (μονολόγιστη). Thus, the simple remembrance within the heart helps retain the unceasing prayer while reason accommodates the simple logismoi –the plain concept of a thing disengaged from passion.

These three states are what the Fathers call purification of the heart. When a person's heart is cleansed he becomes more sociable, balanced. He behaves properly within society, because his selfishness has given way to love for God and love for man. Selfish love is transformed into unselfish love. Formerly, he would love selfishly, with a love which seeks its own. Now, however, he loves with a pure love. He loves others without expecting anything in return. He loves independently of whether others love him. There is no self-seeking in his actions. Thus, when selfish love is changed into unselfish love, one speaks of the person as having become a real human being. And it is this transformation which is considered the cure of man.

In patristic tradition praxis is also called ethics. St. Gregory Palamas speaks of ethics in his texts, he is actually developing the theme of purification of heart. Therein the entire way of man's cure is described. In Orthodox tradition ethics is not an abstract condition, neither is it a pharisaical outward behaviour; rather it is asceticism. Therefore, when the Fathers speak of ethics, they mean asceticism. And since asceticism is a person's passage from impurity of the nous to its cleansing and on to its illumination, orthodox ethics, therefore, is man's purification.

If praxis is the purification of heart in patristic tradition, theoria is on the one hand the illumination of the nous and on the other the vision of the un-created Light. Thus in the teaching of St. Gregory Palamas, it appears that theoria of God is man's union with God. It is effected through divinization (theosis) and bestows upon him the knowledge of God. Theoria –union– theosis and knowledge of God are synonymous terms in patristic tradition.

This is the path leading to a person's cure. Just as every science has a specific way of guiding a person to knowledge, so also does the Church have a method to lead man to God. And this method consists of purification of the heart, illumination of the nous and divinization (theosis) – also called praxis and theoria.

6. Sacraments and Asceticism

Orthodox spirituality is Christ-centred and Church-centred. This means that man is sanctified and saved through the God-man Christ, living within the Church which is the blessed Body of Christ. Christ does not exist outside of the Holy Trinity and outside of the Church. For this reason living within the Church, which is an infirmary and Hospital, we can be cured.

Participating in the uncreated grace of God and experiencing ecclesiastical life are effected through the Sacraments and ascetic practice. Through the Sacraments, the uncreated grace and energy of God enters our heart; through ascetic practice on the one hand, we prepare the way of God's grace to act therapeutically and redemptively within the heart; on the other hand we safeguard divine grace which we received through the sacraments.

St. Nikolaos Kavasilas, in his book "On the life in Christ", analyses extensively that a person's rebirth is accomplished in the mysteries; however our co-operation (synergy) is also needed. God's energy is offered through the mysteries: Baptism gives man his identity with and hypostasis in Christ; Chrismation perfects the newly-born, granting him inner direction; Holy Eucharist maintains and keeps the vitality and well-being that man has received[22].

---

22. See St. Nikolaos Kavasilas, The Philokalia of the neptic and ascetic Fathers (in Greek), ed. Gregory Palamas, Thessaloniki 1979, Vol. 22, pp. 278-288

If the energy of God is offered through the Sacraments, synergy –the response to this great gift– is a matter of our own eagerness and indulgence. Thus God operates and man co-operates. Our own ascetic endeavour is, then, required so as to safeguard divine grace. Kavasilas refers to this subject also, in one of the chapters, entitled "How grace received through the sacraments, is preserved".

The significance of the sacraments, by way of which we receive divine grace, is therefore very great. Nikolaos Kavasilas says that the "Sun of righteousness" enters our darkened world, as if through a small window; this worldly life, He revives the world beyond. All the Saints of our Church refer to this collaboration between sacraments and ascetic practice. I would like however to refer more extensively to the writings of St. Gregory Palamas[23].

First of all St. Gregory emphasizes that the mysteries (mystiria in Greek) are called such because they are spiritual and hidden, and not simply something to be perceived outwardly. Thus, when one approaches the sacraments he must focus not only on what is seen outwardly but also on what is visualized within –at the spiritual level.

To continue, St. Gregory maintains that Baptism is not enough; one must observe the commandments of God, in other words, practise the ascetic life. The ascetic life though is not solely for monks, but it is the keeping of the commandments of God by all followers of Christ. Our endeavour to put into practice God's

---

23. See St. Gregory Palamas, Greek Fathers of the Church (in Greek, Ε.Π.Ε.), Thessaloniki 1986, Vol. 11, p. 406

commandments constitutes asceticism in Christ[24]. After his resurrection Christ said to his disciples: "Go ye therefore, and teach all nations, baptizing them in the name of the Father, and of the Son, and of the Holy Ghost: Teaching them to observe all things whatsoever I have commanded you" (Matt. 28, 19-20). This is why St. Gregory stresses that Baptism does not suffice to make man a disciple of the Gospel; the keeping of the commandments of Christ is also necessary.

St. Gregory Palamas is a universal (catholic) theologian and Father of the Church. Moreover, all the Fathers of the Church are catholic, in the sense that they do not hold one-sided views, autonomous positions. They do not overrate one part of the truth at the expense of another, but rather they maintain a spiritual balance, precisely because they have been renewed by the Holy Spirit. The catholicity of Saint Gregory is made manifest in his stance on two heretical claims of his era, regarding sacraments and asceticism which distorted the spiritual life.

The first claim was expressed by the Massalians, ancient heretics whose ideas were revived during the time of St. Gregory. According to their teaching, the sacraments of the Church, –holy Baptism and the divine Eucharist– are not of such great importance for man's salvation. They claimed that that which unites a person with God is the so called noetic prayer. It is prayer which cleanses man and accomplishes his divinization (theosis) –not the sacramental life.

The second heretical claim comes, primarily, from

---

24. See St. Gregory Palamas, Greek Fathers of the Church (in Greek, Ε.Π.Ε.), Thessaloniki 1986, vol. 10, p. 476

Western Christendom, as expressed by the philosopher Barlaam at the time of Palamas. Barlaam, with whom St. Gregory was in dialogue, greatly emphasized the sacramental life of the Church at the expense of the hesychastic life. He despised hesychasm and everything having to do with noetic prayer. For Barlaam participation in the holy sacraments of the Church was the ultimate act. Barlaam did speak also of prayer but in an abstract and reflective manner. Moreover, he emphasized that the grace of God is created and that the theoria of God is the vision of created light. In general, he disdained and spoke mockingly of the hesychastic tradition of the Church, which is the very foundation of all dogmas and the shared life of all the Fathers.

St. Gregory Palamas undertook a comparable struggle against both heretical claims. He maintained, just as the Church does, that the excessive emphasis on the part of one claim and undervaluation on the part of the second, regarding the truth, constitutes a divergence from the Orthodox life and consequently distances man from salvation. He stressed that for a person to be cured (and consequently for his salvation) a combination of both the sacramental and ascetic life is needed. The hesychastic way of life cannot be thought of outside of the sacramental life of the Church.

Thus, according to the Hagiorite Saint, the therapy of the soul is achieved through both the sacramental and hesychastic life. Outside this combination it is impossible for Orthodox life and Orthodox theology to exist.

In many of his homilies, St. Gregory refers to the great significance of the sacraments of the Church. In one such homily he teaches that Christ sanctifies man's hypostasis and grants the remission of sins "through the divine Baptism, the keeping of His commandments, the repentance which He grants to sinners; and through the transmission of His flesh and blood". It is these two basic sacraments of the Church –Baptism and the Holy communion– together with the observance of the commandments of Christ that afford the remission of sins and sanctify man. Through Holy Baptism, Christ becomes the Father of humanity, and through Divine Communion, He becomes their Mother. St. Gregory makes use of a simile by saying that Christ "feeds us just as a loving mother breast-feeds her infant". He takes the analogy further by saying that the two "nurturing breasts" (of the Church and of the Christ) are Holy Baptism and Holy Communion, the two most essential sacraments.

In another of his homilies, St. Gregory Palamas refers again to the power of these two sacraments by explaining that Christ assumed a human nature and therefore, like us, He had a soul and a body. He suffered through the passions, death and burial and then was raised from the dead; and in this manner, He made it possible for us to partake of the bloodless sacrifice and enjoy our salvation. Through the soul's descent into Hades and her return, Christ imparted eternal light and life; and as a token of this He gave us Holy Baptism[25].

Soul and body are sanctified by these two sacraments; our salvation depends on them. It is obvious therefore that St. Gregory Palamas sees a person's salvation as dependent on one's participation in the

---

25. See St. Gregory Palamas, Greek Fathers of the Church (in Greek, E.Π.E.), Thessaloniki 1986, Vol. 11, p. 444

holy sacraments of the Church. He does not underestimate their importance, like the Massalians did, but he considers them as the centre of the spiritual life. He analyses each one of the sacraments extensively in many of his homilies.

However, St. Gregory does not stop here with the emphasis only on the worth of the Church sacraments. As was pointed out earlier, participation in the sacraments must be combined with the practice of the ascetic life of the Church. Otherwise, the grace transmitted through the sacraments does not contribute to one's salvation or cure but rather to one's punishment. For this reason, Palamas also refers to the hesychastic life concurrently with his teaching on the sacraments.

Grace is granted freely through the sacraments, to those people who have properly prepared themselves. We are ultimately unworthy of this gift but he has rendered us worthy "out of unworthiness". It is necessary, however, for us to co-operate by offering our repentance[26].

St. Gregory employs examples from the Old Testament to underscore this truth. In their journey to the promised land, the Hebrews were tempted by evil desires, and thus the "forms of sacraments given to them" did not benefit them. God abandoned them and they did not enter the promised land. Exactly the same will happen with Christians. Baptism and the other sacraments will not deliver them from eternal damnation, if they live without repenting and do not observe the divine commandments.

---

26. See St. Gregory Palamas, Greek Fathers of the Church (in Greek, E.Π.E.), Thessaloniki 1986, Vol. 11, p. 406

In another passage he says that the Holy Spirit, being of equal might with the Father and the Son, freely "flies to and away from" (i.e. in an act of free will). In other words He remains with repentant sinners, but flees from the impenitent, as happened precisely to Saul, who lost God's grace. This is why he who partakes of the sacraments must live in a state of repentance[27].

As described by St. Gregory, asceticism consists of living the hesychastic life, which is the way of a person's therapy. Presenting the Mother of God as the model hesychast, the Saint analyses extensively that one's goal is to attain theosis, i.e. communion and union with God. This is accomplished by his effort to mortify his reasoning, his senses, his imagination and vain glory, and to focus his nous within his heart, and through his heart for his nous to ascend toward God. Thus Holy Baptism makes a person like "a new born infant", who is graced with latent wisdom, which must later be actualized. The regenerated man through Holy Baptism has received the power to become "a partaker" in the glory of God, yet only if he lives in truth this new life and upholds the Gospel of Christ.

What has been discussed up to now, has clearly demonstrated that the practice of the sacraments and asceticism, concurrently, is indispensable. It is the teaching not only of St. Nikolaos Kavasilas and of St. Gregory Palamas, but also of the tradition of the Orthodox Church. A spirituality which is not based on this foundation is not Orthodox. Moreover, through

---

27. See St. Gregory Palamas, Greek Fathers of the Church (in Greek, Ε.Π.Ε.), Thessaloniki 1986, vol. 10, p. 482

the Sacraments, divine grace is dispensed, according to the condition of our souls. Thus one person may be cleansed by divine grace; another is illumined, while still another may be deified. Because of these teachings, an Orthodox Christian is very cognizant of the link between the sacraments and the stages of the spiritual life; his alliance demonstrates the close relationship between the sacraments and ascetic practice.

The tradition of the Church is very explicit on this point. Two examples follow: the first, "Baptism and asceticism" and the second, "divine Eucharist and asceticism".

In the ancient Church a whole preparatory period preceded the Baptismal ceremony, in order for the Catechumens to approach this "first of Mysteries" as worthily as possible. As it can be seen in the liturgical tradition and the works of the holy Fathers, there were two classes of Catechumens. The first was the "advanced" class. The people who had received the faith but had yet not been baptised belonged to it. They participated partially in the prayers of the Church, after receiving the priest's blessing. The second class were the ones not yet fulfilled–the observers. They would remain in the narthex of the Church up until the reading of the Scriptures and then they would have to leave the temple. In some cases the first category of Catechumens might be relegated to the second category, if an action was deemed as transgressive. Thus the pastoral care of the Catechumens was quite thorough. The Church was very mindful on this point.

Characteristic is the manner in which new members were received; and this was determined by the Second Ecumenical Synod.

According to this edict, on the first day they are called Christians, with a prayer read, relevant to the occasion. On the second day, they are classified into the Catechumens; on the third exorcisms are read and the Catechumens are taught the faith. Afterwards, they are advised to remain in the Church in order to listen to the Holy Scriptures; and finally they are baptised.

The above decree viewed in comparison with the teachings of the holy Fathers and the practice of the Church, asserts that Catechesis is not simply a theoretical initiation into the matters of faith, but it is a complete liturgical act and method of cure. In St. Cyril of Jerusalem's teaching of the faith, the Catechumens are advised to confess before Baptism. He then asks them to take part in the exorcisms, which were read continually. He finally admonishes them to participate in the teaching of faith. And through all these means they should be able to cleanse their heart.

The period of Catechesis lasted from one to three years. It could be shortened though depending on the particular circumstances.

After Baptism, ascetic practice followed, signifying that Christians were to apply the will of God in their lives, as noted earlier. Apart from this, if there were baptised Christians who fell into serious sins –demonstrating that they were not living members of the Church– they would relapse in fact to the Catechumens stage. Certainly, the mystery of Baptism would not be performed again, but, the stage of repentance would have to be repeated. In general, the Church defined four stages of doing penance.

In the first stage there were those who sat outside the temple asking for mercy. In the second stage they remained in the church, attending the divine liturgy until the scriptural readings, and then leaving together with the Catechumens. The third stage included those who followed the entire divine Liturgy while on their knees. The penitent of the fourth stage stayed until the end of the divine Liturgy, together with the faithful, but did not take Communion. Finally, after having passed through all these stages successively, the penitent could partake of the undefiled mysteries; of the Body and Blood of Christ. This step by step description is noted in the Canons of St. Basil the Great.

This procedure is emphasized in the Canons of the Church, because sin is considered a malady and fall from communion with God. It is first and foremost the darkening of the nous, and consequently repentance is the cure and illumination of the nous. When St. Basil the Great designates a certain period of abstinence from holy Communion, he does so for the cure of the "ill" person. This is why he stresses in epigrammatic fashion: "Cure is not conditioned by the passing of time but rather by the manner of repentance". In any case, it is evident that ascetic practice is necessary both before and after baptism.

The same also holds true for holy Communion, the partaking of the holy gifts.

Spiritual struggle and asceticism are needed before holy Communion. St. Nikolaos Kavasilas underscores the toil preceding holy Communion, when he comments on the words of Christ: "Labour not for the meat which perisheth, but for that meat which endureth unto everlasting life, which the Son of man shall give unto you" (John 6, 27) and the words of the Apostle Paul "if any would not work, neither should he eat" (1 Thess. 3, 10)[28]. If we need to work hard in order to gain the "food which perishes" so much so for divine Communion. Christ, through the sacraments, becomes our ally. An ally does not give a hand to the slothful and the bored, but to the strong and the bold, who face the opponent bravely and well. Yet, even after holy Communion we need ascetic practice in order to preserve the divine grace received through the sacraments. Reading the prayers carefully after holy Communion reveals this. The faithful servant prays to God for repentance, tears and strength so that he will remain a true member of Christ. He also implores the Mother of God to mediate to her Son for contrition and compunction of heart.

Consequently, ascetic life is necessary prior to and after divine Communion. The grace of God received through the partaking of the Body and Blood of Christ acts according to a person's spiritual state. If a person finds himself at the cleansing stage, divine grace purifies him, if at the state of illumination, it illumines him; and it deifies him even more, when approaching divinization (theosis). Thus, holy Communion becomes purification, illumination and theosis. Yet, when a person is not repentant or even in the process of purification, holy Communion becomes fire and condemnation; its effects torment.

In conclusion, the significance of combining the sacraments and ascetic practice is manifest throughout all of Church tradition. Their separation creates misconceptions and distortions of the spiritual life, and this is contrary to Orthodox spirituality.

---

28. See above St. Nikolaos Kavasilas, Vol. 22, pp. 452 -454

7. Neptic and Social Theology

Theology in its authentic expression is the word of and about God. The more theology is bound to the truth and to the vision of God, the more the word about God is true. This, however, presupposes the presence of a true and faithful theologian. In the teaching of the holy Fathers of the Church, the theologian is identified with the God-seer. Only he who has seen God and has been united with Him through theosis, has acquired the true knowledge of God. According to St. Gregory the Theologian, theologians are those who have reached "theoria", having been previously cleansed of their passions; or being at least in the process of purification.

It is precisely this position that reveals that the theology of the Church is one, and that there is no separation into neptic and social theology. All theology is simultaneously both neptic and social. This signifies that the holy Fathers are also not sharply divided into neptic and social theologians.

Nevertheless, a conventional distinction can be made in speaking about the Fathers who lived all their life in the desert and those who were engaged in pastoral service. Yet, it should be said that even this distinction is contrived for two basic reasons: firstly, because even the alleged social Fathers passed through "nepsis"* (watchfulness) and purification of the heart; and secondly, because the neptic Fathers, who lived as hermits practised pastoral service indirectly: through their prayers for all the world and by guiding pilgrims who visited them in order to be healed.

The true work of theology is the cure of the person. A real theologian knows the problem and is able to cure it. And, certainly, the actual sickness itself is the darkening of the nous. Thus, the true theology is neptic, and the real theologian is in essence neptic, since he must recognize all the secrets of the spiritual struggle and have discernment, which has been cultivated as a result of his own spiritual journey to health.

Hence, all of Orthodox theology is neptic, since it aims at man's cure. It cures man and liberates his nous from the tyranny of reason, of the environment and of the passions. This is accomplished by watchfulness and prayer.

Watchfulness (nepsis) is attentiveness, spiritual alertness. Christ said to his disciples: "Watch and pray" (Matt. 26, 41). The Apostle Paul also instructs his disciple Timothy: "watch thou in all things" (2 Tim. 4, 5). Thus, watchfulness is spiritual attentiveness; it is the readiness of the nous not to accept any alluring thought. According to the holy Fathers, watchfulness (nepsis) is the presence of reason at the gateway of the heart, guarding against the entry of temptation

---

*Nepsis (watchfulness): Spiritual alertness, constant attentiveness and readiness so that the thought won't progress from the reason and enter into the heart. It is only the nous that must be within the heart and not the thoughts-logismoi. This spiritual alertness is called nepsis.

and the creation of any precondition that might result in committing a sin. Watchfulness is closely related to prayer. According to St. Maximos the Confessor, watchfulness keeps the nous clear of any tempting suggestion, whereas prayer brings rich grace into one's heart. This is why watchfulness is also called the sentinel of the heart. Thus, watchfulness and prayer, in other words attentiveness and prayer are the two spiritual weapons which constitute "philosophy in Christ".

Practical philosophy, of which St. Maximos the Confessor speaks, is not theoretical speculation, but inner noetic work through which a person becomes a proper instrument of divine Revelation. It is in this way that man becomes a bearer of Revelation and knows God. The heart is freed from all thoughts-logismoi and retains only one utterance, –the unceasing prayer, "Lord Jesus Christ, Son of God, have mercy on me, a sinner".

The heart does not accept any other "logismoi". Rejection of logismoi does not mean, of course, that reason is severed from one's thoughts, but rather it is the deliverance of one's nous, i.e. his heart. This is how the heart is cleansed and through prayer receives much grace from God. This whole process is called noetic hesychia-hesychasm. Hesychasm is nothing else but the spiritual "method" through which the heart is cleansed so as to retain only the name of Christ within.

And precisely this activity takes on, at the same time, social character, for, when man is treated, he becomes at once the most sociable of men. When a society, a family is made up of healthy people severe social or family problems are practically non-existent.

Perhaps, due to individual circumstances or the temperament of each person problems may arise, however a cured person recognizes what can be overcome and puts things in order. This can be seen in certain ascetics, who retain shortcomings, due to illness, age or their character, yet even these defects seem "graceful", i.e. do not provoke; they are considered as natural manifestations of a man who has the uncreated grace of God within him.

Accordingly, by establishing certain points it can be disclosed that the neptic man is the social man par excellence.

a) The greatest and most significant social act in the history of humanity, was accomplished by the Mother of God. The Theotokos as She is referred to in the Orthodox Church did not claim any office in the first Church. She did not minister, as the Apostles did. Rather She occupied herself with silence and prayer. Nevertheless She rendered a great pastoral service.

St. Gregory Palamas says that after Christ's Ascension into Heaven, the Theotokos lived with patient endurance and many ascetic practices, praying for the whole world and admonishing the Apostles, who preached in the universe. For the Apostles the Theotokos was a pillar of support whose prayers they hearkened to and whose insights and contributions to the preaching of the Gospel they embraced. Thus, through her prayer and co-operation with the Apostles She helped, most significantly with the work of mission[29].

The work of the Theotokos, though, is not con-

---

29. See above St. Gregory Palamas, Ε.Π.Ε., Vol. 10, pp. 442-444

fined to this area only. The Panagia (the Saint above all Saints) became the greatest missionary in history, for She prepared herself and reached divinization– theosis in the way She knew; She became "the most blessed" and in the end became worthy of begetting the Son and Word of Son. She gave her flesh to the Second Person of the Holy Trinity in order for Him to be incarnate. She, therefore, on the one hand, showed us the path we must follow if we desire to draw near to the likeness of God; on the other hand, She offered to us the most powerful medicine for our illness: namely, She became the cause of the greatest happiness the world will ever know– She gave birth to the incarnate Christ.

This great work is beheld, of course, in the lives of the true hesychasts, as well. By being involved in the purification of their own hearts and the cure of their own personalities, they offer great comfort to humanity. The regeneration of just one person can give rise to the greatest clamour in all the universe. The hesychasts bear testimony throughout the ages to the work of missions by their mere existence, their prayers and teachings. They bless and sanctify the world even after their death, through their holy relics. Thus it is within silence that the most dynamic action takes place.

b) The person who is regenerated by divine grace becomes the most sociable being of all. A good ex- ample of this is the parable of the prodigal son, as interpreted by St. Gregory Palamas[30].

Possession and sustenance is our nous. When our nous relies on God, we are in a good state. Yet, when

---

30. See above St. Gregory Palamas, E.Π.E., Vol. 9, p. 92

we open the door to our passions, then our nous "spreads" itself around and wanders constantly in the direction of worldly things, various pleasures and impassionate thoughts. On our way it lures us away from true love, the love for God and love for our neighbour, and toward the desire for worthless things and the longing for vain glory. This is how love of pleasure, greed for money and ambition develops. Then, the person is taken ill, as St. Gregory Palamas expresses it, he becomes unhappy, and neither the sun's radiance nor the breathing in of fresh air, gives him pleasure.

The "prodigal" nous, i.e. estrangement from God, has consequences not only for the individual whose debasement has made him ill, but also for the whole society; for he becomes enraged and fights against his fellowmen because his unreasonable desires cannot be satisfied. He becomes homicidal and he comes to resemble a wild animal.

Therefore, when one's nous is estranged from God a person becomes anti-social, whereas when the nous returns within the heart from its dispersion and then ascends to God, he becomes all the more social. A cured person is the health of his community.

c) It follows that the person who is a bearer of Orthodox spirituality is inwardly integrated. He does not succumb to the tyranny of thoughts-logismoi*. And it is well known that logismoi can create dreadful psychological problems, driving a person to insanity.

When we speak of logismoi we do not mean just simple thoughts but those rational suggestions as-

---

*See Footnote p. 56

sociated with images and stimulations brought on by sight or hearing or by both together. Logismoi, therefore, are images and stimulations with an intrinsic suggestion. For instance, an image comes to our mind concerning glory, wealth or pleasure. This image is accompanied by a thought: "if you do this, you will gain glory, money –you'll be very powerful". These rationalizations are called logismoi and through their power of suggestion can evolve into sin.

"Coupling" is man's conversing with the logismos, yet still hesitating whether or not to act upon it. "Assent" is a step beyond mere coupling. Man resolves now to act upon the specific logismos. Desire comes in the process and the commitment of sin is effected. Repeated acts of sin create passion. At the stage of coupling, the logismos aspires to incite pleasure so as to captivate the nous and consequently, to enslave the person.

According to the Fathers, the logismoi are either simple or complex. A simple logismos is not obsessive, whereas a complex thought is linked with passion and a concept. St. Maximos makes the distinction among passion, concept and object. Gold is an object, just as a woman or a man. The simple memory of an object is a concept. And passion is irrational love or random hatred attached to the concept of a particular object.

Logismoi evolve into sin and passion. And passion is not only born of logismoi but also strengthened by them. It acquires powerful roots and afterwards a person experiences great difficulty in his own transformation. One's logismoi literally makes a person decay. They poison and defile the soul. Logismoi bring turmoil to the soul's faculties. The holy Fathers not only attribute a person's downfalls to logismoi, but also describe the disturbances they cause in interpersonal relationships. Moreover many physical illnesses are caused by the unrestrained presence of logismoi. Beyond all of this, however, a man possessed by logismoi loses his candour and intimate communion with God.

Whoever follows the path of cure properly is freed from logismoi; he becomes inwardly balanced and behaves normally. He neither torments himself nor others. This is very significant for if we observe people who are psychologically imbalanced, we can see clearly that they are possessed by fixed ideas and patterns of thought and are unable to free themselves from them.

d) Neptic life is social life; and it is in fact social life par excellence, because it helps a person to reclaim the natural faculties of his soul and to function, from this point on, "according to nature" (i.e. as God intended).

In the teachings of the holy Fathers passions are not outside forces which enter us and must thus be uprooted. Rather they are energies of the soul which have been distorted and need to be transformed.

A person's soul as far as the passions are concerned is divided into three faculties: the intelligent (reasoning), the appetitive (desire) and the irascible (affective). These three faculties must be directed toward God. When they turn away from Him and others, they become known as passions. For this reason, passion is movement of the soul contrary to nature.

St. John the Sinaite makes this quite clear by using certain examples. Conjugal relations are quite natural for procreation; however contemporary man has altered their significance into something banal. Anger is natural when directed against the evil one, however we use it against our brothers. Jealousy is natural as long as what is coveted and emulated are the virtues of the saints. However, this also gets employed against our brothers.

Desire for glory is inherent provided it is the kingdom of Heaven that is sought but unfortunately this desire is expended on trivial, temporal and mundane things. Pride connected with glory is natural when turned against the demons. Gladness is natural when it is in Christ. We have received rancour from God to use it against the demons. We have received the inclination for true extravagance, which is related to the desire for the wealth of eternity. Yet, we turn this into squandering. Thus the passions are the movement of the soul's faculties contrary to nature.

Within the perspective of Orthodox spirituality when a person is liberated from self-conceit, which begets worldliness, avarice and ambition, he acquires love for God and love for men. He truly loves others. He sees in each person the image of God. And for this reason he becomes truly and social. Who can deny the fact that the person himself is the one who corrupts social institutions, and in turn these corrupted social institutions make people all the more disfunctional. When an unwell person assumes a position of authority, he creates enormous social problems.

An exception is the one who lives in the hesychastic tradition, being himself transformed, becomes a comforter to others who have problems and are tormented by them.

e) One of the greatest existential, as well as social problems is death. It afflicts everyone by its very existence or when it touches our loved one. Death is terrible for man, because it disrupts the unity between soul and body and the union among beloved persons. It is the source of sin. Not only is it the offspring of sin but it also causes sin.

Man is born mortal and perishable. Consequently, he must inevitably face the exigencies of illnesses and the eventuality of death, which definitely creates great insecurity. Man actually experiences death when he tries to succeed in his life, to make his name, to earn a lot of money or to be insured in the best insurance companies and to be liked by many people.

"Let not sin therefore reign in your mortal body, that ye should obey it in the lusts thereof" (Rom. 6, 12).

"The string of death is sin" (1Cor. 15, 56)

"But I see another law in my members, warring against the law of my mind, and bringing me into captivity to the law of sin which is in my members. O wretched man that I am! who shall deliver me from the body of this death?" (Rom. 7, 23-24).

Another consequence of the decay and mortality in our nature is the passions of avarice and love of possessions. When a person experiences the tragedy of death in his more intimate environment, by losing one of his beloved persons, he feels its impact. He falls into despair and depression.

The tragedy of death becomes more intense as a person feels himself steadily approaching it. If he does not believe in God it is difficult to overcome the painful moments that ensue.

The Christian, however, who lives the ascetic and

sacramental life of Orthodox spirituality, overcomes mortality. Through Baptism and holy Communion he moves beyond his biological existence and acquires the well-known spiritual hypostasis. He has communion with the Saints and is well aware of the existence of the Church triumphant, and that death has been abolished by the resurrection of Christ. He knows that there is also another life into which he will enter to live eternally in the love of God, beyond mortality and decay. He also knows that the bodies will be resurrected.

Some people claim that the Church is not involved in any social deeds. This is not true, for the Church exercises a rich and varied range of social work. If we investigate carefully we will discover that there are the local Archbishops and priests who develop various programs, comforting the poor, the abandoned, the elderly, the sick, the orphans etc. Apart from this, however, we must say that the Church's greatest social offering is that she is there to help man overcome death. Cannot the loss of a beloved person cause such a disruption within a family, that nothing can compensate for it? And is this not one of the gravest social problems?

Moreover, as was stressed earlier, the mortality and decay in our nature generates a multitude of social problems, creating the desire for wealth, possessions, etc. The Church, through its shepherds, liberates man from these tormenting problems. She prepares him to cope with death with alertness, composure, and above all with faith in God.

On the Holy Mountain one meets monks who do not fear death, as happens with all the Saints. In his description of the death of St. Antonios, St. Athanasios says that after the brothers who were present, embraced St. Antonios, the Saint, being overjoyed stretched out his legs and "fell asleep".

f) The healed and healthy person also cultivates all other cultural values. Our Church's Saints left us an eminent cultural legacy –an offspring of their own sanctified personality: magnificent churches, monastic institutions, renowned in their time as well as in ours, iconography not easily reproduced by the contemporaries, superb hymnography of exquisite literary value, in addition to their deep faith and devotion; music appreciated by the great musicologists of our times. The person who is spiritually healthy produces "healthy" works –the fruits of his own regeneration.

g) Because the bearer of Orthodox spirituality loves God and understands through his illumined nous the causes of beings, in other words he sees the uncreated energy of God in all creation, he treats nature and all the world properly. Thus one might also say that he contributes to the solving of the often referred to ecological problems.

Today overconsumption is creating the demand for overproduction. This excessive production has immense consequences for the earth, which is being violated for this purpose. It is no wonder then that a ravished nature, is "punishing" the inhabitants of earth. This pollution of the environment is not independent of the passions of pleasure-loving, avarice and ambition. Today nature suffers more as a result of its oppression under the dominion of impassionate man. Now more than ever the ascetic way of life is a need.

The spiritual exercises of the Orthodox Church, as

previously described, have a beneficial effect on the surrounding world. This is seen in the lives of many Saints who respected nature exceedingly; not just emotionally did they love nature, but because they could see, through their purity, the energy of God in all of creation. Such cases are abundant on the holy Mountain:

"Once I needlessly killed a fly. The poor thing crawled on the ground, hurt and mangled, and for three whole days I wept over my cruelty to a living creature, and to this day the incident remains in my memory.

Somehow it happened that some bats bred on the balcony of the storeroom where I was, and I poured boiling water over them, and once again I shed many tears on this account, and since then I have never harmed any living creature.

One day, going from the Monastery to Old Rus-sikon-on-the-Hill, I saw a dead snake on my path which had been chopped into pieces, and each piece writhed convulsively, and I was filled with pity for every living creature, every suffering thing in creation, and I wept bitterly before God.

The Spirit of God teaches the soul to love every living thing so that she would have no harm come to even a green leaf on a tree, or trample underfoot a flower of the field.

Thus the Spirit of God teaches love towards all, and the soul feels compassion for every being, loves even her enemies and pities even devils because they have fallen away from the good". (Archim. Sophrony, St. Silouan the Athonite, Stavropegic Monastery of St. John the Baptist, Essex 1991)

Moreover, it is known that nature does not have a

moral will. Consequently, it did not fall by itself but was swept along to decay by human beings. Adam's sin had immense consequences for nature too. For this reason every person's sanctity or sin reflects on creation, too.

Therefore, Orthodox spirituality is both neptic and social. And it is precisely because it is neptic in the fullest sense of the word that it can be social. The experience of community outside of the neptic life is in reality unsocial.

8. Monasticism and Married Life

Orthodox spirituality is accessible to all people; responding to its message is not associated with special groups of people. All those who have been baptised in the name of the Holy Triune God are "compelled" to uphold Christ's commandments. There are no exceptions on the way toward theosis, which is the "journey" from the image of God to His likeness. The Apostle Paul says clearly: "For as many of you as have been baptized into Christ have put on Christ" (Gal. 3, 27).

The essence and aim of Orthodox spirituality presented in the foregoing chapters is delineated in the Word of Christ and the teachings of the Apostles. Many passages from Holy Scripture have been quoted which show that the first Christians lived the spiritual life profoundly, having attained to the illumination of the nous and unceasing prayer.

In a reference to virginity and marriage the Apostle Paul states: "He that is unmarried careth for the things that belong to the Lord, how he may please the Lord: But he that is married careth for the things that are of the world, how he may please his wife" (1 Cor. 7, 32-33). Yet, at the same time he stresses: "But this I say, brethren, the time is short: it remaineth, that both they that have wines be as though they had none" (1 Cor. 7, 29). Thus married people also lived ascetically and had experiences of the spiritual life.

Moreover, not to be overlooked is the fact that all

of the Apostle Paul's Epistles, sent to the various Churches, were addressed to Christians who were married and had families. And it is within these Epistles that St. Paul speaks of cleansing of the heart, illumination of the soul, acquisition of noetic prayer, of the unceasing prayer of the heart, Sonship by grace, and of life in the Holy Spirit. These epistles disclose that the Christians of the first Apostolic Churches lived as the monks live today in the holy monasteries.

When the persecutions ceased, however, and Christianity became the official state religion, secularization penetrated the Church and the ascetic way of living disappeared from the cities. It was precisely *during this time that monasticism developed* as an attempt to preserve the essence of the spiritual life. For this reason the holy Fathers emphasize that monasticism is the continuity of the Apostolic age and the life of the first Church; and that the monks are those who live the life of the Gospel, who experience repentance to its ultimate degree and who try to observe the commandments of Christ unyieldingly. Every Orthodox monk who lives within this atmosphere is an Apostle of Christ, a Martyr and a Prophet. Monasticism is apostolic, prophetic and martyrial life.

To understand the essence of monastic life, one should read the beatitudes of Christ. The monk commences his life in profound repentance with tears of mourning and the cleansing of the heart. In the Gospel and the Apostle Paul's Epistles all the elements which constitute the genuine monastic tradition, as proclaimed by the Fathers, can be found.

These same elements are emphasized in the service of monastic tonsuring. It states there that during the noviciate period the prospective monk passes through the stage of the Catechumen, living in deep repentance and undergoing purification of the heart. This is the "first love" of which the Evangelist John speaks in the book of Revelation. When repentance is accomplished monastic tonsuring takes place, which is referred to as the "second baptism".

Monastic tonsuring is called a mystery because the monk experiences the purifying and illuminating energy of God. According to St. Symeon the New Theologian the second baptism is the baptism of the Spirit, that is, the illumination of the nous and the acquisition of noetic prayer. The following is said to the monk while he is being tonsured: "You are purged of your sins and becometh son of light". Thus, the monk experiences purification of the heart prior to his tonsure, and acquires illumination of the nous while being tonsured.

The apostolic life and the way of life of the first Christians, as described in the Pauline Epistles and the book of the Acts, is made visible.

Monasticism is apostolic and evangelical; mortification of the "old man" precedes it, though, and then the monk becomes a "temple" of the Most Holy Spirit. The prayers read by the priest are expressive of this theme.

Married Christians in their personal lives are also called to live the Gospel and the commandments of Christ. Noone is exempted from this responsibility. Every one must experience repentance; overcome selfishness; and acquire love for God and love for others.

It is apparent that the circumstances of married life are different from those of the monastery, and thus a certain adjustment is needed. Yet, what the monastery is for the monk, the family is for the married person. Family is the place for ascetic practice in married life. It is therein that a person is called to carry out the will of God.

"O God most pure... bless this marriage, and vouchsafe unto these thy servants, N. and N., a peaceful life, length of days, chastity, mutual love in the bond of peace, long-lived seed, gratitude from their posterity, a crown of glory which fadeth not away. Graciously grant that they may behold their children's children. Preserve their bed unassailed, and give them of the dew of heaven from on high, and of the fatness of the earth. Fill their houses with wheat, and wine, and oil, and with every beneficence, that they may bestow in turn upon the needy; granting also unto those who are here present with them all those petitions which are of their salvation". (Rite of the Holy Matrimony)[31].

The Church has placed all of its teaching on marriage in the prayers read during the marriage ceremony. The wedded are blessed to live their lives in love and prudence, following the commandments of God.

"Be thou exalted, O Bridegroom, like unto Abraham; and be thou blessed, like unto Isaac; and do thou multiply like unto Jacob, walking in peace, and keeping the commandments of God in righteousness.

And thou, O Bride: Be thou exalted like unto Sarah; and exult thou, like unto Rebecca; and do thou multiply, like unto Rachel: and rejoice thou in thy husband, fulfilling the conditions of the law: for so is it well-

31. Service Book of the Holy Orthodox-Catholic Apostolic Church by Isabel Florence Hapgood, New Jersey 1975, 5th ed., p. 295

pleasing unto God". (Rite of the Holy Matrimony)[32].

The fact that women and men who had been worthy of experiencing divine vision in the Old Testament are mentioned in the prayers, demonstrates the ascetic and saving character of marriage in Christ. The holy Fathers teach that conception, gestation and birth constitute the "garments of skin" which Adam wore after the Fall. God, however, eventually blessed this way. St. Maximos writes that marriage, as we know it today, is a result of the Fall[33].

St. Chrysostom teaches that all of the commandments of the Gospel –except, of course, for that of marriage– are to be shared by all men –monks and married[34].

St. Basil discerns that both –monastics and the married– are called to uphold the commandments of Christ in the Gospel.

St. Gregory Palamas, on the theme of the purity of the heart, declares that married persons can also strive to attain it[35].

The existence of many married Saints who possessed noetic prayer both in the Old and the New Testaments reveals that married people have the capacity to experience Orthodox spirituality in all its manifestations. The prophetess Anna kept noetic prayer within her heart and prayed unceasingly while in the midst of experiencing great pain.

---

32. Hapgood Service Book, p. 300-1
33. See St. Maximos the Confessos, PG 90, p. 788
34. See St. Chrysostom, PG 57, pp. 81-82
35. See The Philokalia (in Greek), ed. Astir, Athens 1976, vol. 4,
    p. 92

Within the framework of Orthodox spirituality, therefore, Christians are not divided into categories of married and single, monastics and lay people; however they are separated into those who have the Holy Spirit within and those who do not. It is possible for all people to uphold Christ's commandments and experience Orthodox spirituality under the guidance of a spiritual father. There are neither privileged nor non-privileged people within Orthodox tradition.

Conclusion

1. It is not the intention of this book to analyse in detail all aspects of Orthodox spirituality. Rather, the text simply offers an introduction to the fundamentals of Orthodox tradition. The reader should take advantage of the opportunity to refer to other texts, in order to supplement his knowledge on the subject.

2. Explicitly underscored is that the spiritual person is he who partakes of and participates in the energies of the Most Holy Spirit; he, who has himself become a dwelling place of the Holy Spirit. This does not constitute an abstract, emotional or intellectual spirituality. The bearer of Orthodox spirituality par excellence is the Saint who is revealed through his teachings and his relics. The non-spiritual individual, who is deprived of the Holy Spirit, is the psychological and carnal person.

3. It is precisely the above distinction which points out the difference between Orthodox spirituality and other "spiritualities". Orthodox spirituality differs markedly from the "spiritualities" of the East and the West. The difference in the dogma generates the difference in ethos as well. The essence of Orthodox spirituality lies in its therapeutic effects. It cures a person's infirmities and renders him an integrated person.

4. And what is cured first and foremost is a person's heart, which constitutes the centre of his

entire being. In other words, it is not treatment of just the visible signs of illness; it is also the cure of the inner self, of the heart. While ill, a person's nous is dispersed by way of the senses into the world. It becomes identified with the intellect and this is why it must return to dwell again within the heart, which is the work of Orthodox spirituality. The Orthodox Church is referred to as Hospital-infirmary, a clinic of the soul, precisely for this reason.

5. The Orthodox Church, however, does not just stress the necessity of cure; it also outlines the means by which it can be achieved. Because a person's nous and heart are impure, he must pass successfully through the three stages of growth in the spiritual life: purification of the heart, illumination of the nous and theosis. Orthodoxy is not like philosophy. It is more closely related to the applied sciences, mainly to Medicine. This is said in the sense that cure in the Orthodox Church can be substantiated by its results. These three stages of the spiritual life are in reality participation in the purifying, illuminating and deifying energy of God, for they are attained through divine grace.

Apart from this division concerning the spiritual life (purification, illumination, theosis), there is that of praxis and theoria. It is not a matter of a different category, but of the same, because praxis denotes catharsis and repentance, whereas theoria is illumination of the nous and theosis.

7. The cure of the whole person, which is the essential aim of Orthodox spirituality is effected by the sacraments of the Church and by the practice of the ascetic life. A break in the bond between sacra-

ments and asceticism leads to pretentious moralizing or to total secularization.

8. There is no division as well, between neptic and social theology; neither are the holy Fathers divided into neptic and social theologians. "Healthy" sociability is a consequence of the neptic life and nepsis-watchfulness is the foundation of true sociability. Freeing the soul from logismoi, passions and the tyranny of death, makes for a balanced person, psychologically as well as socially. It is in this way that all social, political, ecological and family problems are solved.

9. In the Orthodox tradition no clear distinction is made between monastics and married persons; neither are there different spiritual obligations and guidelines delineated for each group. All can and should keep Christ's commandments in their lives. Monastics and married persons simply differ in the location of and extent of their spiritual practice; the goal is the same. All are called to follow the path which leads to the likeness of God.

10. Orthodox spirituality is Christo-centric because the hypostatic union of divine and human nature was accomplished in Christ, indivisibly, inseparably, and without confusion or change. This is why Christ is the sole medicine of the person's ills. Because Christ cannot be considered independently of the other persons of the Holy Trinity and of the Church which is His Body, Orthodox spirituality is simultaneously Trinitarian and Ecclesiastical at its core.

11. Within the spiritual infirmary of the Orthodox Church the method for curing of the whole person is preserved. Today, still, there are Christians who live the stages of spiritual life: purification, illumination

and theosis. It is from this, that we see the contribution ofhodox Church and Orthodox spirituality. The person who has been healed solves at once all of his existential and social problems.

Other works by the same author

In english:

1. A night in the desert of the Holy Mountain, first edition 1991, reprinted 1994, second edition 1995, reprinted 1998, Birth of the Theotokos monastery, p. 200

2. The illness and cure of the soul in the Orthodox Tradition, first edition 1993, reprinted 1994, 1997 Birth of the Theotokos Monastery, p. 202

3. Orthodox Psychotherapy, first edition 1994, reprinted 1995, 1997, Birth of the Theotokos Monastery, p. 372

4. Life after death, first edition 1996, reprinted 1998, Birth of the Theotokos Monastery, p. 392

5. St. Gregory Palamas as a Hagiorite, Birth of the Theotokos Monastery, 1997, p. 400

6. The mind of the Orthodox Church, Birth of the Theotokos Monastery, 1998, p. 239

7. The person in the Orthodox Tradition, Birth of the Theotokos Monastery, 1998

* * *

In greek:

8. Mia vradia stin erimo tou agiou Orous, editions A' 1978, B' 1979, Γ' 1982, Δ' 1984, E' 1985, ΣΤ' 1986, Z' 1987, H' 1989, Θ' 1990, I' 1992, IA' 1993,

IB' 1994, IΓ' 1995, IΔ' 1997, IE' 1998, Birth of the Theotokos Monastery

9. Osmi Gnoseos, editions "Tertios", Katerini 1985

10. Martiria zois, 1985

11. To Mistirion tis paedias tou Theou editions A' 1985, B' 1987, Γ' 1991, Δ' 1997, Birth of the Theotokos Monastery

12. Paraklitika, editions "Tertios", Katerini 1986

13. Orthodoxi Psychotherapia (Pateriki therapeutiki agogi) editions A' 1986, B' 1987, Γ' 1989, Δ' 1992, E' 1995, ΣΤ' 1998, Birth of the Theotokos Monastery

14. Piotita zois, editions A' 1987, B' 1989, Γ' 1996, Birth of the Theotokos Monastery

15. Apokalipsi tou Theou, editions A' 1987, B' 1992, Γ' 1996, Birth of the Theotokos Monastery

16. Therapeutiki agogi, editions A' 1987, B' 1989, Γ' 1993, Δ' 1998, Birth of the Theotokos Monastery

17. Sizitisis gia tin Orthodoxi Psychotherapia, editions A' 1988, B' 1992, Γ' 1998, Birth of the Theotokos Monastery

18. Psychiki asthenia kai igia, editions A' 1989, B' 1991, Γ' 1995, Birth of the Theotokos Monastery

19. Anatolika I, editions A' 1989, B' 1993, Birth of the Theotokos Monastery

20. Keros tou piisai, Birth of the Theotokos Monastery, 1990

21. To politevma tou Stavrou, editions A' 1990, B' 1992, Birth of the Theotokos Monastery

22. Ecclesiastiko fronima, editions A' 1990, B' 1993, Birth of the Theotokos monastery

23. Prosopo kai Eleftheria, Birth of the Theotokos Monastery, 1991

24. O Vlepon, editions A' 1991, B' 1992, Birth of the Theotokos Monastery

25. Orthodoxos kai ditikos tropos zois, editions A' 1992, B' 1994, Birth of the Theotokos Monastery

26. Mikra isodos stin Orthodoxi pnevmatikotita, Athens 1992

27. O Agios Grigorios o Palamas os Agioritis, editions A' 1992, B' 1996, Birth of the Theotokos Monastery

28. Katichisi kai Baptisi ton enilikon, Athens 1993

29. Romeoi se Anatoli kai Disi, Birth of the Theotokos Monastery, 1993

30. Paremvasis stin sychroni kinonoia A', Birth of the Theotokos Monastery, 1994

31. Paremvasis stin sychroni kinonoia B', Birth of the Theotokos Monastery, 1994

32. AIDS, enas tropos zois, 1994

33. To prosopo stin Orthodoxi Paradosi, editions B' 1994, Γ' 1997, Birth of the Theotokos Monastery

34. Epoptiki Katichisi, Birth of the Theotokos Monastery, 1994

35. I zoi meta ton thanato, editions A' 1994, B' 1995, Γ' 1996, Δ' 1997, Birth of the Theotokos Monastery

36. I Despotikes eortes, Birth of the Theotokos Monastery, 1995

37. Iparxiaki psychologia kai Orthodoxi Psychothe-
    rapia, editions A' 1995, B' 1997, Birth of the Theo-
    tokos Monastery

38. Osoi pistoi, Birth of the Theotokos Monastery,
    1996

39. Gennima kai thremma Romeoi, Birth of the Theo-
    tokos Monastery, 1996

40. Entefxis kai synentefxis, Birth of the Theotokos
    Monastery, 1997

41. Ikonofiliko kai Iconoclastiko pnevma, Birth of the
    Theotokos Monastery, 1998

* * *

42. Secularism in church, theology and pastoral care,
    "The truth", ἀρ. φύλ. 11, 29 Μαΐου - 5 Ἰουνίου
    1994, W. Australia and "Alive in Christ", the
    magazine of the Diocese of Eastern Pennsylvania,
    Orthodoxy Church in America, Volume X, No 1,
    2, 1994, καί Divine ascent, a journal of Orthodox
    faith, exaltation of the Holy Cross 1997, Vol. 1,
    No. 2, p. 10-25

43. Die Autorität in der orthodoxen Kirche (Kurzfas-
    sung der Einführung für deutsche Theologiestu-
    denten am 29.9.1996), εἰς Philia, Zeitschrift für
    wissenschaftliche, ökumenische und kulturelle Zu-
    sammenarbeit der Griechisch-Deutschen Initiative,
    II/1996

44. СЕКУЛАРИЗАМ У ЦРКВИ, БОГОСЛОВЉУ И
    ПАСТИРСКОМ РАДУ, СВЕТИ ГОРА, τεῦχος 68,
    69, 1998

45. ВОСКРЕСЕНИЕ ХРИСТОВО, Крым 1998

ОДНА НОЧЬ
в пустыне
СВЯТОЙ ГОРЫ

Архимандрит Јеротеј Влахос

ВЕЧЕ У ПУСТИЊИ СВЕТЕ
ГОРЕ

МАНАСТИР ХИЛАНДАР

Hiérothée Vlachos
Entretiens
avec un ermite
de la sainte Montagne
sur la prière
du cœur

Traduit du grec par Jean-Louis Palierne

Seuil

HIEROTHEOS VLACHOS

CONVERSACIONES CON
UN ERMITAÑO
DEL MONTE ATHOS

narcea

These books can be found at:

- The greek and english,
  Birth of Theotokos Monastery
  GR - 321 00 LEVADIA, P.O. 107
  GREECE

- The french,
  Éditions du Seuil
  27, rue Jacob, Paris VIe

- The spanish,
  Narcea, S.A. De ediciones,
  Dr. Federico Rudio y Galí, 9. 28039 Madrid.

- The arabic,
  Archéveche Grec Orthodoxe
  Beyrouth, Liban

- The russian,
  Свято-Троицкая Сергиева Лавра
  Перевод с новогреческого
  Художественное оформление

- The serbian,
  Monastery of Chelandari
  Mount Athos, Greece

- The hungarian,
  zöld -S Stúdió (VS STUDIO)
  1535 Budapest, Pf. 699